THE BEST SALES BOOK EVER

CUT

Through the **OBSTACLES** *and*
SEND SALES THROUGH THE ROOF

CONNIE PODESTA AND
MERIDITH ELLIOTT POWELL

STANDOUT Press
Dallas, Texas

The Best Sales Book Ever
and
The Best Sales Leadership Book Ever

Published by:
STANDOUT Press
3308 Preston Rd.
Suite 350-119
Plano, TX 75093

Printed in the United States of America.

Content Development and Editing: Susan Priddy (www.SusanPriddy.com)
Cover Design and Interior Layout: Kendra Cagle (www.5LakesDesign.com)

Library of Congress Control Number: 2019904425

ISBN: 978-1-946225-15-3 (paperback)
         978-1-946225-16-0 (Kindle)
         978-1-946225-17-7 (ePub)

Connie Podesta Presents, LLC
www.ConniePodesta.com
connie@conniepodesta.com

Meridith Elliott Powell
www.ValueSpeaker.com
mere@valuespeaker.com

DEDICATION

To the thousands of salespeople out there who work hard every day. You prospect. Connect. Listen. Offer value. Consult. Overcome objections. Negotiate. Ask for the money. Wait. Worry. Reconnect. Worry some more. And then you feel the ultimate frustration when the deal still falls through. WTH?!?

We get it. We feel your pain. That's why this book is dedicated to you. It's designed to help you better understand the minds of your potential buyers so you can open more doors and close more deals. You're in good hands now. We believe in you. And we've got your back!

TABLE OF CONTENTS

SECTION ONE:
Beliefs that Destroy Sales Potential

SECTION TWO:
Excuses that Get in Your Way

SECTION FIVE:
Negotiation Tactics that Diminish Your Power

INTRODUCTION

Co-Author Q&A
With Connie Podesta (CP) and Meridith Elliott Powell (MEP)

This personal, behind-the-scenes conversation with the authors will give you some fascinating insights into the genesis of this book and its distinct purpose.

Connie Podesta
- *Sales & Leadership Psychology Expert*
- *Hall of Fame Keynote Speaker*
- *Award-Winning Author of 9 Books*
- *Elite Sales Strategist*
- *Comedienne*
- *Executive Coach*
- *Therapist*

Meridith Elliott Powell
- *Business Growth Expert*
- *Acclaimed Keynote Speaker*
- *Award-Winning Author of 6 Books*
- *Master-Certified Business Strategist*
- *Executive Coach*
- *Online Course Instructor*
- *Former Sales Leader*

Q: Tell us about the unique approach you've taken with this book.

MEP: Salespeople today are inundated with articles, podcasts, webinars, and workshops that tell them what to do if they want to increase their sales. They are already overloaded with long lists of things to do and ideas to consider with hopes of closing more deals. So, we decided to look at their challenges from a different perspective. We wanted to turn the tables on this idea of doing more and show them how to be more productive by doing less.

CP: The people who are really achieving the mind-blowing Sales success are the ones who figure out what NOT to do. There's a psychological component that comes into play here. These salespeople have a unique mindset that allows them to let go of the techniques and strategies that aren't working for them. They seem to have a higher sense of self-awareness and self-discipline. Ultimately, they quit doing the things that are holding them back. Not because quitting is the easy way out or because life isn't fair. They just quit and choose to do something else that moves them closer to their goals.

MEP: Here's the challenge. Some people — especially salespeople — may associate quitting with losing. They don't like to give up or give in. They want to hang in there and persevere. That's what has made them successful, so the idea that quitting could actually lead to increased sales may be challenging to understand. But it works. It's a proven fact. Our approach is somewhat unexpected (and sometimes a little irreverent), but it's exactly what they need if they want to improve their results.

CP: We think you'll see that this book is really about more than just quitting. It's about what salespeople will gain when they choose to give these things up. Granted, change isn't easy. But letting go allows them to gain traction and move forward in astonishing ways. We describe exactly how to make those changes with the opportunity for extraordinary impact, both personally and professionally. There's a potentially lucrative payoff for following this advice.

> **Q: What's the bottom line here? Why should salespeople read this book?**

CP: The short answer? Because they want to sell more and make more money. Maybe they want to land larger customers, close bigger deals, build stronger relationships, increase market share, or get the recognition they deserve. Whatever goals they have, this book will give them the secret shortcuts to success in every aspect of Sales.

MEP: Exactly. We cut to the chase in this book and provide Sales strategies in very specific categories. It's all the things salespeople need to quit if they want to be more successful... The beliefs that could be destroying their potential. The excuses that are getting in their way. The faulty assumptions that are costing them money. The negotiation tactics that could be diminishing their power. The things they are doing that keep them busy but prevent them from being productive.

CP: One other point that's important to add. Our goal was to make this a comprehensive guide for Sales professionals, so we recognize that seasoned salespeople are probably already applying some of these strategies. However, we also firmly believe that they will discover some new ones they have never considered. From that angle, this book provides value for salespeople at every level.

Q: Explain the unusual format you've selected.

CP: We've really given our readers two books in one. From this side, they can discover the strategies to help them become extraordinary salespeople. If they flip the book over and read from the other direction, they'll find strategies to become an amazing Sales leader.

MEP: The truth is, the journey toward success is quite different for salespeople versus Sales leaders. There are some commonalities, but we wanted the leadership aspect to share the spotlight as well. Both areas are critically important.

CP: We actually recommend that salespeople and Sales leaders read both sections. That helps Managers review the pivotal skills and behaviors they want to reinforce during their team training and coaching. As for salespeople, they can use the leadership portion of the book as a career planning guide. Either way, having a comprehensive view of Sales and leadership gives people tremendous insights into the overall process.

Q: What makes you the best people to tell this story?

MEP: Between the two of us, we have worked with tens of thousands of salespeople and Sales leaders around the world. This book presented us with an incredible opportunity to join forces and combine our cumulative experience and wisdom.

CP: Definitely. Once we pooled our knowledge, we realized we had a one-of-a-kind collection that covered the topic of Sales from every possible angle. There was a huge need for that kind of thing in the marketplace, and we created a concise, straightforward resource to meet that need. We think our readers will agree that this is the most comprehensive Sales book ever — hands down.

BELIEFS...
THAT DESTROY SALES POTENTIAL

Your sales performance can't soar if some of your mindsets, attitudes, and behaviors are dragging you down.

1

QUIT

UNDERESTIMATING THE IMPORTANCE OF PSYCHOLOGY.

Sales is all about "solving the people puzzle." To be honest, that's basically the key to success in every area of life. But in Sales? You absolutely, positively have to understand what makes customers tick if you want to build profitable relationships and make more money. That's the big differentiator.

Why? Customers today are overwhelmed, to say the least. They are facing the challenges of extreme stress. Corporate change. New leadership. Painful downsizing. (Go ahead, fill in the blank with the *adversity du jour.*) To provide customers with solutions they will be clamoring to buy, you have to dig deep and help them identify what they really need.

Before you can get buy-in, consensus and ownership, you have to get inside your customers' heads. Figure out why they do what they do. Why they say what they say. Why they react the way they react. The more you know about your customers' mindsets, the faster your business will grow. Plain and simple, to get ahead in Sales, you must be committed to understanding the psychology of human behavior.

In case you're rusty on your knowledge about Pavlov, Freud and Piaget, here are three great psychological tips to help boost your Sales IQ:

a. **Customers don't like paying for "stuff."** But they love investing in solutions that allow them to work faster or smarter. Or make more money. If you can deliver results, convenience and cost savings, you'll increase your sales.

b. **Customers like to feel in control.** Let them tell you what they need first; then offer the perfect solution. You can still lead the conversation, but focus on their input. It matters.

c. **Customers prefer avoiding losses more than acquiring gains.** It's a proven principle of cognitive psychology: They want to win, but they REALLY hate to lose. Instead of just telling customers about the benefits they will gain with your product, tell them what they're missing out on.

SALES TAKEAWAY

Learn as much as you can about the nature of human behavior as it relates to Sales. Understanding that psychological angle will help you increase sales, gain market share, and blow away the competition.

2

QUIT

ALLOWING OLD MONEY MESSAGES TO UNDERMINE SALES.

Money isn't everything, and it shouldn't be your first priority when you're working to close a deal. With that said, some salespeople unconsciously reduce their income because of self-limiting beliefs that hold them back. That's unfortunate.

There are always people in our audiences who don't believe they deserve the accolades, awards, attention, or wealth that come with being a top Sales performer. Somewhere along the line, they developed an attitude about money that sabotages their success. Which is a serious problem in Sales. And in life.

Here's the deal: The way you feel about money (positive or negative) probably started in childhood. In most homes, money is a stressful topic. How to earn it, spend it, save it, increase it, and what to do when there's not enough. And of course, who has the power to make those decisions. The underlying messages we absorb related to money can stick with us for a lifetime.

Chances are, those messages have cast money in the role of the villain. Ever heard any of these stereotypical statements? Money is the root of all evil. Money can't buy happiness. People *without* money are deemed to be honest and hard-working, while people *with* money are often labeled as ruthless and uncaring.

Guess what? Money isn't the villain. We can have a wonderful life without tons of money. But let's be honest: Money can add a lot to an already wonderful life! It's all about your beliefs.

If you're going to work your tail off to earn money, then be happy and guilt-free about what it can do for you. Start believing that money is a good thing. It's OK to want it, plan for it, enjoy it, share it, and use it in all sorts of positive ways. On the flip side, it's not OK to chase it, hoard it, idolize it, use it to feel superior, or believe it's the answer to all your problems. Again, your attitude makes the difference.

Don't let those long-held, preconceived notions about money mess with your head as you build your Sales business. If you are uncomfortable discussing money, negotiating your fee, or simply enjoying the financial rewards of your career, it's time to let go of those old messages.

SALES TAKEAWAY

Start now to embrace new beliefs about money based on hard facts rather than fear, anger, prejudice, guilt, or sour grapes. Truly believe that you deserve to be success-ful at Sales and you deserve the wealth that comes with it!

3

QUIT

SABOTAGING YOUR POTENTIAL.

Sales goals can be a double-edged sword. On the plus side, dangling that number in front of us can rev up our engines in a huge way. It can create an enormous incentive for us to hit the pavement, sell like crazy, and work tirelessly to meet the challenge. But what happens once we reach that quota?

We see it all the time: It's like flipping a switch. The salespeople who were working at warp speed to achieve their lofty goals suddenly come to a screeching halt. Complacency takes over. And you can bet that tragic loss of momentum has consequences. Not only have they quit trying to help their customers and their companies, but the dead stop also puts serious limits on their income.

The most successful salespeople adopt the attitude that Sales is more of a lifestyle than a task. Of course, you will always have goals to meet, but don't let those become the driving force behind everything you do. To be successful in Sales, you need to embrace the fact that there are endless ways to sell. To explore new opportunities. To generate new income streams. To discover new revenue sources.

Take us, for example! We've had a great track record speaking professionally to Sales audiences (and make great money doing it). But that doesn't mean we are sitting back and taking it easy. No way!

We are both constantly looking for new opportunities to market, expand, and revitalize our business models. What else could we offer? What services could we provide that would blow our competitors out of the water? How can we come up with innovative ideas that will astound and excite today's competitive Sales teams who think they've heard it all?

With that in mind, be honest. Are you fired up to do more? Or are you just going through the motions? Feeling so secure in your job that slacking off doesn't even bother you? Most importantly, do you think no one notices? (Brace yourself: They do.)

If you want to boost your career with additional business, don't allow yourself to coast. Resist the urge to relax once you meet your Sales quota. There's always *more* out there.

SALES TAKEAWAY

Refuse to sabotage your potential by becoming complacent. Goals and quotas have an expiration date, but Sales is an ongoing process. Keep pushing forward, no matter how great your progress looks on the spreadsheet!

QUIT

SELLING WHAT YOU DON'T BELIEVE IN.

Successful salespeople need a wide range of skills, and *confidence* is certainly one of them. But they also have to genuinely believe in what they are selling. Why? Because most customers have an inner radar detector that can smell manipulation and game-playing a mile away!

If you don't believe in what you're selling, neither will they. Which brings up a less-than-pleasant side to the Sales industry. Sad to say, there are some salespeople out there who can look potential customers squarely in the eyes and brag about the brilliance of products they know perfectly well are low quality or even defective. They are willing to deliberately mislead, exaggerate, fail to disclose, or outright lie to seal the deal. That's completely dishonest and just plain wrong.

Don't be one of those people!

To determine whether you are a true believer in your product, ask yourself some targeted questions:

a. Will the product deliver what you are promising?
b. Will it actually meet your customers' needs?
c. Is it unique compared to the alternatives?
d. Will its quality stand the test of time?
e. Will the company back it up if something goes wrong?
f. Would you buy this product yourself or sell it to someone you cared about?

That last question is pivotal. When you sell this product, you're essentially endorsing it — which means your professional reputation is on the line. Whether you realize it or not, your willingness to sell a certain product sends a strong message about your principles. Your values. Your integrity. That choice isn't random; it really matters.

If you wouldn't buy it, you're developing Sales relationships that are built on deceit and manipulation. But if you really believe in your products, your customers will believe in you. They'll see your sincerity and enthusiasm, and they'll respond in positive ways. Every time. That brand of passion will open doors, close deals, and help you surpass the highest goals. Now that's a win/win for everyone!

SALES TAKEAWAY

Great salespeople develop customers based on a foundation of trust and integrity, so make sure you believe in the products or services you sell.

5

QUIT

PERPETUATING THE SILO MENTALITY.

For the Sales leadership perspective on this chapter, see page 43 in the reverse side of the book.

As a salesperson, you may end up with a narrow perspective of what you can provide for your potential buyers. After all, it seems like a basic formula. The company creates a specific set of products or services, and you are sent out to find buyers. What you see is what you sell. Right? Not so much.

Those perceived limitations often seep in when salespeople suffer from the silo mentality. They start to believe that the Sales department is its own island, operating independently at the end of the organizational spectrum. And that's a HUGE roadblock for success. Continuing to maintain that myopic view not only limits what you can sell, but also what you can earn.

The good news? Those limitations aren't real. But if you want to offer your customers additional value, you'll have to break out of the silo mentality to do it. As we often tell our audiences, there's no force stronger than several departments collaborating toward a single, aligned vision.

To harness that power, try applying these three strategies:

a. **Adopt a team perspective.** Expand your thinking to consider the bigger picture. Who else within your organization has an impact on the quality of the customer experience? Your co-workers are creating the product quality you rave about in Sales meetings, defining the price points you tout to prospects, and offering the follow-up services that give customers the confidence to buy from YOU. This is a team effort, not an individual race.

b. **Find ways to join forces with your colleagues.** Could you provide customer input to help the development team make subtle yet powerful product improvements? Could you brainstorm with the distribution team about untapped delivery options that would beat your competitors? Could you work with Customer Service to help them pinpoint problems so you can respond with more effective solutions?

c. **Make it a habit to communicate across silos.** Be willing to suspend your ego and express the desire to learn from others. The reality is, someone outside of Sales could hold the key to a new offering that excites, impresses or satisfies your customers. You CAN offer your customers more value; it's just up to you to find it.

SALES TAKEAWAY

Be willing to drop the silo mentality to offer your customers more value. You'll discover a wealth of new resources and ideas that can lead to greater money and increased success. Totally worth it!

6

QUIT
IGNORING THE POWER
OF PERSONALITY.

While most personality assessments end up categorizing individuals in one of four distinct groups, salespeople may find value in a more streamlined view. No test or #2 pencil required.

Generally speaking, the world is filled with people who either tend to be more concerned about the bottom line or more concerned about relationships. There's a vast spectrum, of course, but most personalities naturally gravitate to one side of that line or the other. While that might sound like an overly simplistic view, it may provide incredibly rich insights for those in Sales.

How does it work? The first step is to determine the more dominant trait for your own personality. Are you a cut-to-the-chase salesperson who relies on the facts and arrives at conclusions in the most direct manner? Or do you prefer the scenic route that explores the important feelings and emotions behind every decision? Neither one is wrong, by the way. It's just important to recognize your usual mode of operation.

The second step is to identify which of those two personality types best describes your potential buyers. The signs will be obvious, so listen and watch for clues. Bottom-liners will take charge immediately and expect prompt answers about deliverables and pricing. The relationship buyers will want to start by chatting a bit and getting to know you.

Here's why that matters. When you're dealing with people who tend to operate the same way you do, you'll make a faster connection. You'll just feel like you're on the same page. The other half of the prospect population might present a bigger challenge. In those cases, the key to success is following the lead of their personality styles and conversational-flow preferences.

Resist the urge to sell according to your own natural tendencies. Instead, sell in a way that's most comfortable for your customers. For bottom-liners, get right to the point and make your pitch. For relationship-builders, take your time. Understanding the power of personalities will make all the difference in the world for your Sales performance.

SALES TAKEAWAY

Accommodate the personality styles of your buyers to maximize your success. That never means being inauthentic, but simply recognizing their preferences for personal interaction. Customers are more likely to do business with people who can do business their way.

7

QUIT

BELIEVING THAT CLOSING MORE DEALS WILL MAKE YOU HAPPY.

What's the tipping point for you to actually feel *happy*? Some salespeople view happiness as the RESULT of getting everything they want. Closing more deals. Increasing sales. Expanding market share. Getting a better territory. If you're patiently waiting for happiness to show up after you earn enough and accumulate all you need, get ready to settle in for a long, long wait.

Let's redefine happiness. It is NOT the RESULT of getting what you want. That's an unfortunate myth. Happiness is the CATALYST that makes getting what you want possible. Happiness has to come first! Reality check: If you are unhappy, you will never truly succeed in Sales.

Why? Because your attitude, personality, and sense of engagement aren't at a level that attracts customers who are willing to buy. Being happy generates all the perks; being unhappy…doesn't.

We know what you're thinking: That's a steep road to climb. How can you be happy when clients are rejecting you? When the well of leads is running dry? When deals are painfully slow to close?

No magic bullet on this one. The solution is to suck it up and start *acting happy*. It's a fake-it-'til-you-make-it experience. Remember that selling from a place of happiness is sometimes your only shot at attracting the kinds of clients, deals, success, and profits you truly want in your life.

Believe me, we've "acted" our way into happiness mode more times than we can count when life was falling apart around us. Still do. Why? Because we want the bad stuff to end. And the good stuff to start again. ASAP! And we know that adding some happiness to the mix gives us the best chance to level the playing field and turn things around.

Be brutally honest with yourself. If you're not totally happy, what are you waiting for? More money? Better clients? Bigger deals? Your lack of happiness might actually be what is pushing those goals out of reach. It's time for a change! Make the *choice* to be happy, and you'll have a much better chance of getting exactly what you want.

SALES TAKEAWAY

Recognize the psychological link. At its deepest level, Sales is about attraction — the chemistry between you and your customers that allows them to trust you and turn to you for business solutions. Work to radiate happiness, and your customers will naturally be more attracted to you.

8

QUIT
THINKING SALES CAN BE MASTERED.

Sales is like golf: There's always room for improvement. Just when you think you've got the game down to a science, you find yourself in the rough trying to escape with your dignity intact.

One of the biggest mistakes we see from salespeople is believing they've "reached the top." They are skeptical about exploring new paths toward success because, according to them, they know it all. The reality? Those are usually the salespeople who are stuck in outdated patterns of selling the same old way. Oh yes, precisely the folks who need to upgrade their skills.

Time to debunk the myth of mastering Sales. There's always more to learn. New approaches to pursue. New strategies to implement. New techniques to be applied.

No matter how high your sales numbers get, you're still leaving money on the table. *Somewhere. Somehow.* Guaranteed. Sales is a lifelong endeavor based on continuous improvement.

We are always shocked by the number of salespeople who never take advantage of FREE training resources and tools offered by their own companies. Why not? That's just foolish. The moment you quit learning about Sales is the moment you become irrelevant.

Think about all of the factors that impact Sales: customer preferences, innovation, the economy, competition. Each of those elements remains in a constant state of change, which means salespeople have to shift as well.

If you want to master the art of selling, commit to staying at the top of your game with continuing education. Reading this book is an excellent start! Search for professional development opportunities that can help you remain on the cutting edge of Sales techniques and strategies that are proven to deliver success. Never get complacent about the need to make learning an ongoing activity.

As part of that education process, regularly take note of your own Sales behaviors. Reassess what's working and what's not. And just try to be open to new ideas and tactics that will continue ramping up your skills (and your results).

Sales is most definitely not a discipline that can be mastered. On the upside, you can position yourself as a perpetual student of this craft. That commitment will be the fuel to keep you moving forward in search of increasing levels of excellence within your career.

SALES TAKEAWAY

Invest the time and energy each week to learn more about Sales. The "top" doesn't exist, so keep reading articles, blogs and books; attending Sales conferences; and shadowing other Sales professionals. There's always room for improvement!

EXCUSES...
THAT GET IN YOUR WAY

Fastest way to
boost your sales?
Start taking ownership.
And stop confusing
excuses with
legitimate reasons
for not closing deals.

1

QUIT

BLAMING THE PRODUCTS.

Think about the power of choice. You CHOOSE the company you work for. Through that decision, you are CHOOSING to sell within a certain industry or product category. Which makes it interesting when your excuse for poor performance comes down to, *"I just don't like what I'm selling."*

Seriously?!

Here are the questions you need to address: If you don't like these products, why did you take the job? Why would you deliberately choose to make yourself miserable all day, trying to convince other people to be excited about a product that bores you to tears? Are other salespeople reaching their quotas? Maybe those "boring" products have become a convenient scapegoat.

Admit it: Maybe the problem is YOU. And guess what? Blaming the products isn't moving you anywhere but backward. If you want to move forward, you'll need a serious attitude adjustment. Reconnect with your purpose. Generate some enthusiasm. Find something to love about your products and your job.

With that said, let's step back and look at the reality of product apathy.

Sometimes hopeless products really do deserve the blame. (Shout-out to anyone stuck selling push lawn mowers and transistor radios!) And we also understand that products change. Quality drops off. Support diminishes. What you're being asked to sell today isn't necessarily what you signed up for on Day One.

If that's your situation and you no longer believe in what you're selling, it's time to move on. Refuse to listen to the people who keep telling you, *"Get back out there! A great salesperson can sell anything."* When the passion for what you are doing is gone, exercise your power of choice and share your talents elsewhere.

SALES TAKEAWAY

Take a deep look inside and be honest with yourself. Find the root of the problem. Whether it's your assigned products or your attitude, fix it — or change it. No more excuses.

QUIT
BLAMING THE PRICE.

"I didn't make the sale because our prices are just too high."

Guess what? That's not a valid excuse. The reason customers choose NOT to buy goes way deeper than price. Cost is just the easiest to blame. If you're losing the sale because of price, you aren't really selling!

So what's the problem? How can you determine if blaming the price of your product has become a bad habit whenever you can't close the deal? Take a closer look at the anatomy of your Sales process, and ask yourself some candid questions.

Are you *only* selling the price? You're basically training your customers to think of your product as a commodity. Which is a huge problem when your competitor offers a special deal or finds a creative way to trim costs. Every customer interaction will be laced with fears that a cheaper price will end the relationship.

Are you selling *price* rather than *value*? People are willing to pay more if they believe they are getting more. Help your buyers see the benefits of what you have to offer from a broader perspective. It's your job to demonstrate that the cost of the product aligns with the value that the customer will receive.

Are you selling a *product* rather than a *solution*? When you can show customers exactly how your product meets their unique needs, price becomes a secondary consideration. Think about the "pain points" they are experiencing, and identify how you can help to relieve those. Beyond your product. On a larger scale. Be a consultant first and a salesperson second.

Are you projecting *confidence* in your product pricing? Price discussions often make salespeople nervous. Their voices and body language change. They start looking down. Talking faster. Making excuses. It's like they are apologizing for the cost before they ever ask for the order. If customers don't believe what you're selling is worth the price, why should they buy? Fully understand how your product can add value, and describe it with confidence as you explain the pricing structure of your offering.

SALES TAKEAWAY

Be confident about the value your product delivers and the needs it can fulfill. When you stop selling price, you'll start closing more deals. Guaranteed.

3

QUIT

BLAMING THE TERRITORY.

Salespeople have ways of making the territory excuse sound completely plausible.

"My territory is too small."
"The market is already saturated."
"Too many competitors in this area!"
"This region doesn't have the right buyers for my products."

But guess what? You may be creating a self-fulfilling prophecy. Whatever you tell yourself about the limitations of your territory will likely become a reality. In other words, the big Sales problem isn't your territory; it's your *perception* of that territory. If you convince yourself there's not enough opportunity in your market, you'll be right! And there never will be.

Reframe the way you think about it:

a. **Remove the expectations.** Every territory is different. Your job as a Sales professional is to crack the code. Ditch the one-size-fits-all approach, and figure out the best strategy to sell within your market parameters.

b. **Stop thinking that "small" is bad.** In our experiences, smaller markets often have distinct Sales advantages over larger, urban areas. You don't have to travel as far to meet people face-to-face. You can plug in to the community more easily and make valuable contacts. Plus, advertising and communication are cheaper. It will probably cost less to reach more of your potential customers with better marketing materials.

c. **Sharpen your Sales strategy.** Instead of declaring that your territory is too big, too small, too competitive, or just too tough, develop a customized plan to help you achieve success in that specific environment. Have you invested time to learn about your territory? Who are the top targets and influencers? Any hidden gems? What should you focus on or avoid?

SALES TAKEAWAY

Remember that every territory requires its own Sales approach. Don't complain about the puzzle; solve it! (Hey! That's what makes Sales one of the most interesting jobs around.) Invest the time to learn about your territory, and then create a plan to generate Sales success right where you are.

4
QUIT
BLAMING LACK OF LEADS.

———

Closing new customers may be your first priority, but that can't happen without quality prospecting and lead generation. Your ultimate success depends on finding people who need your specific product. People who want your product. People who can afford your product. If you can't start your Sales process from a list of people who meet those criteria, you'll be wasting a lot of time and energy.

Make it a priority to do your part in the lead-generation game. Implement some strategies to better prequalify your own leads or do whatever you can to support the people who find them for you. Here are some tips to help you maximize your Sales leads:

a. **Get to know your Marketing team.** Especially if these folks are generating leads for you! That's a time-saving luxury many salespeople don't have. Learn more about their process, and explain what you need. If they don't know what's working and what's not, they can't improve the quality of the leads they provide.

b. **Follow up on the leads you get.** Sounds obvious, right? Statistics actually show that at least half of leads generated are NEVER contacted. What's that all about?

c. **Update your customer profile.** As your organization develops new products and services, consider whether your target has shifted. Make sure you align your contacts with the new qualification process.

d. **Reevaluate your CRM.** Is there a better way for you to optimize it? Does it need an upgrade – or a significant change?

e. **Keep an open mind.** Be proactive and prequalify leads, but don't make rash assumptions about who will buy and who won't. Great salespeople suspend their judgment and confidently tackle the tough clients.

f. **Make customers happy.** Word-of-mouth promotion is powerful, and customers quickly spread the news about their complete satisfaction (or lack of it). We both use this approach for 90% of our lead generation. Your reputation really matters.

g. **Ask for referrals.** Your clients should be happiest at the moment you deliver your products or services. Use that opportunity to inquire about the needs of their colleagues and coworkers.

h. **Don't forget about old leads.** Just because they weren't interested before doesn't mean they aren't now. Remain vigilant about staying connected.

SALES TAKEAWAY

Take responsibility for lead generation, even if you have people assigned to that task. Treat every lead like a seed for success. Some may take a little longer than others to grow, but you never know which one will end up bearing the most impressive fruit.

5
QUIT
BLAMING THE PAPERWORK.

We get it. Nobody really loves filling out forms, submitting reports, or preparing recaps of meetings. It's exhausting to tackle endless emails and paperwork. In the world of Sales, all of those "necessary evils" distract from your primary focus on nurturing leads and closing deals. Worse yet, if you're selling on commission, the time and energy you pour into administrative tasks can chip away at your profit margin.

The response is typically procrastination, immediately followed by additional stress. Papers piled high on the desk start to topple over. Unread emails are filling the in-box. Expense reports are overdue. Co-workers are irritable about unanswered requests.

That's when we tend to hear this comment: *"Hey, I'd love to close more deals, but I'm stuck in the office filling out forms."*

Blaming the paperwork is just another excuse for avoiding the hard work of hitting the pavement and selling at full force. Don't fall into that trap!

To help you move past this common excuse, check out these helpful tips:

a. **Be selective** about when you handle paperwork, avoiding times that are ripe for making sales.
b. **Use sales automation** whenever possible.
c. **Gather context** so you understand the reasons WHY you are collecting certain data.
d. **Take ownership** in the outcomes and impact of the reports you produce to avoid feeling resentful.
e. **Create insights** by reviewing the reports for opportunities to improve the Sales process.
f. **Get organized,** and stay focused rather than trying to multi-task.
g. **Save your energy** for making the next sale rather than complaining about the administrative headaches.
h. **Just do it** — turn off your phone, grab some coffee, and get it done.

SALES TAKEAWAY

Remember that even the greatest jobs involve some less-than-enjoyable tasks. Commit to getting your paperwork done as quickly as possible so you can move on. Or work with management to update and streamline the process. Coming up with a better way could definitely make you a hero.

QUIT
BLAMING LACK OF TIME.

Being busy comes with the territory of being in Sales. Attending meetings that drag on and on. Preparing high-stakes presentations. Working with existing customers on service issues. No wonder you don't have time to increase your sales, right?

Wrong. In our experience with thousands of Sales professionals, we have witnessed that time isn't actually the issue. The heart of the problem involves the *management of time*. We've discovered that's one of the biggest challenges for salespeople to master.

Here's the good news. Regardless of your current Sales level, you probably have the time and the resources today to accomplish more than ever before. Technology has dramatically increased the efficiency of selling, from lead generation to customer communications. Face-to-face Sales meetings can be supplemented with emails, texts, and cell-phone calls made from anywhere in the world. Essentially, these advances provide you with *more* time to sell. To prospect. To follow up.

To help you corral the clock, answer these questions:

a. **What is more important than selling?** Nothing! If you are in Sales, you are responsible for generating revenue. The organization can't exist if it doesn't sell products or services. That needs to be your top priority in managing your time.

b. **What can you offload?** It's one of the very first issues we address with salespeople when we coach them. What can you delegate, automate, eliminate, or outsource?

c. **How are you allocating your time?** Look at your calendar. How much time do you spend with customers (current and potential)? In contrast, how much time do you spend with people and tasks that aren't generating revenue? Long coffee breaks and idle chit-chat in the hall can suck up more time than you realize. If you can shift just one hour per day into the revenue-generating category, you can move from "busy" to "productive" and increase your results ten-fold.

d. **How many things are you doing at one time?** Contrary to popular opinion, multi-tasking isn't really a viable, time-management solution. It actually fragments your focus and undermines your efficiency. Don't do it! Give your full attention to one thing at a time.

SALES TAKEAWAY

Step back and analyze the structure of your day. Prioritize the buyer, and commit to being accountable for each and every hour you devote to the Sales task.

QUIT
BLAMING BAD LUCK.

If you're losing at the slots in Vegas, you might claim to have bad luck. But if you're striking out in Sales, you can't use the same excuse. Blaming bad luck for poor Sales performance is just another way of saying: *"I'm not willing to work my tail off and do what it takes to lock down a deal."*

Let's be clear. Sales has absolutely nothing to do with luck. It's about hard work. Really, really hard work. Every day.

It's about prospecting when you're tired. Studying for hours to know the features and benefits of your products. Generating leads when you'd rather be doing anything else. Making appointment after appointment to solidify one contract. Building relationships when you can't smile another second. Listening to excuses when you know you have the right solution at the right price. And being rejected even though you did everything right.

Sales is a super-tough, anything-but-random job. And some people aren't prepared for that — or aren't willing to put in the effort.

Inevitably, that's when someone chimes in with this statement: *"Seriously, I was just in the right place at the right time. Total luck."*

When you think about it, doesn't that apply to every deal you close? You were there. They needed what you had to offer. They liked you and trusted you enough to buy from you. No one else showed up to offer a better deal. You made the sale. So you can either chalk that up to luck — or recognize that it's a consequence of your cumulative efforts and dogged perseverance.

The statistics tell the story. Which salespeople close more deals? (Hint: Luck isn't part of the equation.) It's always the ones who work harder, reach out to more customers, follow up more frequently, and build more relationships.

Commit to solid preparation and a sustained effort in your Sales process. Leave the impact of chance to the folks out in Vegas.

SALES TAKEAWAY

Make your own luck. Be consistent about doing the things that are proven to generate Sales success. And when you do them over and over again, you'll repeatedly find yourself in the right place at the right time.

8

QUIT
BLAMING THE MARKETING TEAM.

The blame game isn't exactly uncommon when Sales teams and Marketing departments clash. In fact, we can often predict the dialogue between these two, intrinsically intertwined groups.

Sales:

"We aren't getting the kind of leads we need to close deals."

"Have you seen our marketing materials? So outdated!"

"We'd all make more money if they'd just do their jobs and stop obsessing about our digital presence."

Marketing:

"We give Sales great leads, but they don't follow up."

"They never do their homework to fully understand our products or technology."

"They make the sale and move on. We end up losing customers who feel neglected."

It's an organizational nightmare that needs to stop. If you're in Sales, you have an opportunity to help bridge the gap between these two groups and, ultimately, provide better service to your collective customers.

To make your job easier, consider reaching out to Marketing with these "olive branches":

a. **Give more feedback.** Gently speak up if something's wrong, but show your enthusiasm when they get it right. It might be tempting to make snide remarks on the phone or complain about them behind their backs, but keep it positive.

b. **Be friendly.** Don't enter a discussion ready to aim, shoot, and fire. Remain calm, and give them the benefit of the doubt. Work on the relationship just as you would with a customer. Being open and easy to work with will pay off. Big time.

c. **Define your shared goal.** Be prepared to discuss what a qualified lead looks like to you, and come to agreement about the process: when leads should be followed up and how the cycle should flow. Flexibility is an asset.

d. **Provide targeted input.** If your promotional materials are less than optimal, graciously approach your Marketing team with ideas about improvements that will better resonate with buyers. Message adjustments. Image changes. More compelling statistics. You have the benefit of frontline customer access, so your perspective could be helpful. Just adopt a positive, collaborative tone when sharing it.

SALES TAKEAWAY

Remember that a barrier between Sales and Marketing undermines the whole organization's ability to achieve goals. Take the first step in reaching out to your Marketing colleagues. Positive change can start with YOU — no finger-pointing or taking sides.

9

QUIT

BLAMING THE ECONOMY.

———————

It never fails. Headlines about stock market fluctuations prompt salespeople everywhere to shield themselves with that news. *"I could easily be exceeding my monthly quota if it weren't for the economy. The sales funnel collapsed. People just aren't buying right now."*

After decades of working with Sales organizations in good economic times and bad, we've noticed one important thing. Every industry has salespeople who can close deals right and left during an economic crisis or a financial boom. Whether Wall Street is trading at all-time highs or experiencing epic struggles.

What's their secret?

First, the stellar salespeople refuse to use a sagging economy as an excuse to stop selling. Even in bad times, people still have to buy products. They might not buy as much, but businesses still have to run and families have to survive.

Second, these salespeople toss out the "woe is me" thinking when their 401(k) accounts take a dip. They keep the emphasis on the customers, who may want to vent about their own money issues. Somewhere, woven into those candid discussions, is information about the problem customers are trying to solve in the current situation. Smart salespeople listen carefully to find that underlying message and act swiftly to become the heroic problem-solvers to meet their needs. The byproduct? Building customer relationships that won't budge when Wall Street has a bad day.

Third, great salespeople don't coast and become glorified "order takers" during prosperous economic times. They realize that customers may have extra money on their hands, which could make them ready to restock, upgrade, and innovate. Instead of viewing a bull market as a chance to kick back, they see perfect timing to make bigger sales and expand their presence in the market.

SALES TAKEAWAY

Adopt recession-proof Sales strategies. Help customers solve problems during tough times, and help them invest wisely in growth when the economy flourishes. No excuses. No blame. Just flexible tactics that can lead to a profitable forecast.

ASSUMPTIONS...
THAT COST YOU BIG BUCKS

If jumping
to conclusions
is your daily exercise,
you're leaving money
on the table.

1

QUIT

ASSUMING NEW CUSTOMERS ARE MORE IMPORTANT THAN EXISTING ONES.

Mountain climbers love a tough challenge. But after the celebration of reaching the summit, they're ready to move on to the next mountain. Climbing the same one seems pointless.

Sound familiar? In Sales, the focus always seems to be on *new* customers. Whenever we coach Sales teams, that's the topic people ask about most often. What are the tips and strategies for winning *new* business? They assume that's the real secret to success.

Naturally, no one would argue that new business isn't important, but there's another angle to consider. One of the fastest ways to grow your portfolio and expand your customer base is to focus more of your time and energy on your *existing* customers.

Why? Because you've already done the heavy lifting with this group. They know you. They like you. They trust you. Which means they are primed and ready to buy even more from you with less effort!

Unfortunately, many salespeople put current customers at the bottom of the prospecting list, like a mountain they've already

41

climbed. And when they make that choice, they neglect to keep these customers in the loop about new products, additional services, and updated technology. That's money left on the table.

The mindset of "deal closed, move on" is definitely one to avoid. The last thing you want is for YOUR customer to find out about new offerings from ANOTHER salesperson. Don't let that happen!

Consider it your job to *continue* selling to current customers. Keep them on track. Help them find ways to improve. Strengthen those relationships. And when the time comes for them to add on or upgrade, you'll be perfectly positioned to expand your sales.

And one more thing. The happier you make your existing customers, the more referrals they will send you. Happy customers like to talk and tweet about the experiences that helped to grow their businesses. If you are responsible for those gains, your best source of new prospects could come from your existing customers.

SALES TAKEAWAY

Make it a habit to sell to your existing customers first. That's often the easiest and most productive way to increase your sales and generate new leads.

2

QUIT

ASSUMING PROSPECTS
AREN'T IN A POSITION TO BUY.

Back in the day, we both waited a few tables to make ends meet. Talk about the ultimate Sales job! Customers aren't *obligated* to leave a tip. So, for restaurant servers, the quality of their income is driven by the quality of their service. Cause and effect in its purest form.

We both learned early on that it wasn't in our best interests to adjust our service based on assumptions about which customers were more likely to be big tippers. More often than not, those guesses were wrong. The people we felt "didn't look the part" might leave a huge tip, while the upscale diners with designer handbags might stiff us. Yeah, the don't-judge-a-book-by-its-cover rule still applies.

One of the greatest Sales mistakes of all time is to assume the customer is not in a position to buy. Once you've chosen to believe they don't have the time, money, motivation, or authority to close the deal, where do you go from there? You got it — nowhere.

It starts innocently enough.

"It's Friday. Why bother? He's mentally checked out for the week."
"They just bought new equipment, so I'm sure all the budget dollars are gone."
"Nobody wants to make a decision right before the holidays."
"The competitors have been bad-mouthing us, so I'm sure they won't talk to me."

These excuses are bathed in the mentality of assumptions. If you've had those thoughts, you're leaving money on the table. Even worse, you're leaving the door wide open for your competitors to swoop in and make the sale regardless of the day, season, or situation. The fact is, you're getting in your own way, and you aren't even giving your customers a chance.

Stop trying to talk yourself out of making the sale before you ever get started. Clear out the false assumptions, and adopt the attitude that there's never a wrong time to buy. Even on a Friday. During lunch. On a holiday. At the end of the fiscal year. Whatever it is, don't assume it's a bad time. That's your perception, not theirs.

If you can provide value and helpful solutions, you have everything you need to tap in to your customers' desires and budgets.

SALES TAKEAWAY

Convince yourself that the best time to sell is…NOW! Don't allow your potentially inaccurate assumptions about the buyer to create a roadblock that holds you back.

3

QUIT

ASSUMING YOUR COMPETITION WILL STAY THE SAME.

If we asked you to name your biggest competitors, you would probably start listing the same businesses that you've been competing against for the past five years. Hard truth? That involves the assumption that things are staying the same. And they're not.

This is your stop-burying-your-head-in-the-sand moment.

The competitive landscape can change radically, sometimes even overnight. Traditional competitors make adjustments. Non-traditional competitors dive in with innovative alternatives, many of those online. Or new technology takes a sledgehammer to the whole thing and creates a wildly different way to help customers meet a particular need.

That constantly shifting marketplace leads to major changes in everything from product design and manufacturing to marketing strategies and shipping. Even how people buy and sell!

Think about the impact of progressive companies like Uber and Airbnb. If the equivalents of those companies haven't already invaded your industry, you can bet they are just around the corner.

And they're ready to grab market share if you overlook them.

What does this mean for you as a salesperson? Don't get too comfortable with your perfectly crafted value proposition. Even if you're selling like crazy today, don't assume that your formula for success is timeless. It may not continue to work as well when competitors pop up out of nowhere and change the game.

Sure, it's hard to compete in a world where you have no idea what's coming next. Pay attention to what's happening in your industry and the world at large.

Make sure you are listening closely to your customers rather than serving them on auto-pilot. If you are consistently working hard to understand and meet their needs, they won't be tempted to look for alternatives. When you can turn your buyers into loyal customers with world-class service, you'll be much less susceptible to the unexpected threats made by your competitors (current and future).

SALES TAKEAWAY

Pay close attention to the competitive evolution. Whether you recognize it or not, it's transforming your business every day. No matter what changes, the key to making the sale is still about your ability to meet a customer's needs better than any other option.

4

QUIT

ASSUMING CUSTOMERS ARE HAPPY WITH THEIR CURRENT PROVIDERS.

One of the hardest objections for salespeople to overcome is often delivered with a comment like this: *"Sorry, we've been doing business with a different supplier. They're great."*

That's when it sets in. The punch-in-the-gut feeling of coming face-to-face with a closed, locked door. Quickly followed by the urge to cross that prospect off the list and move on to the next one. At least you tried, right? Hold on there, partner.

Let's back up and analyze this. What did you really expect? Of course, they are already using someone else. They aren't just limping along, trying desperately to run a business without products or services they need. They haven't been sitting around waiting for you to come rescue them. *Everyone* is already working with someone else. That shouldn't even be viewed as an objection. Not for an instant.

And yet, think about how the brain tends to translate the completely expected fact that this customer already has another supplier.

They don't want me or need me.
They're happy with the current situation.
They don't want to make a change.

Really?! They never said that. It's just a cascade of assumptions piled on top of the truth. In reality, they offered you the perfect invitation to pitch your product. You might be able to provide them with something better, faster, cheaper, or more innovative.

To be fair, people don't love the hassle of changing vendors. It's awkward. It might seem like a lot of trouble. They'd rather stick with something they know (even if it's not optimal) rather than bet on the unknown. But these are all objections you can overcome.

Let them know you're thrilled they are satisfied with their current supplier, and you'd still be happy to share a few tips and solutions that might add value. Provide information. Ask questions. Listen carefully. Chances are, you'll help them uncover some very good reasons for making a switch. At the very least, you'll be the first person they call when the current vendor drops the ball. And that WILL happen! Sell to be their second choice and — more often than not — you'll eventually win the business.

SALES TAKEAWAY

Show potential customers what they're missing by working with the same vendor. Give it a try! And don't let your assumptions snuff out the Sales process before it ever starts.

5

QUIT

ASSUMING BUYERS WILL
REMEMBER WHAT YOU SAY.

The buying process puts customers and prospects smack dab in the middle of a factual hurricane. The requirements. The budget. The choices. The specs. The upgrades. The competitive bids. With that whirlwind of information swirling around in their brains, no wonder they seem rushed and overwhelmed.

It's actually amazing that they can remember our names, let alone what we sell and why it's the best option.

Yes, we want to devote time to building relationships. We want to dazzle them with irresistible product features. We want to ensure they intimately understand the reasons why they should work with us. But wait — there's one more aspect we can't afford to ignore.

If we want to put ourselves ahead of the competition, we can't assume our customers will remember everything we say. It's OUR responsibility to remind them. To make their jobs easier. To provide them with "prompts" that will keep our messages fresh. To follow up regularly and stay top-of-mind.

Here are a few hints for helping your customers remember you and your products:

a. **Always take notes.** Ask your customer first for permission to document your meeting. Then write everything down so you have details about what *they* said and what *you* offered.

b. **Share the information.** Immediately after the call or visit, provide the customer with a brief recap to confirm you are on the same page about what took place and include reminders about next steps.

c. **Communicate regularly.** Demonstrate your follow-up and organizational skills. With each contact, you have the opportunity to reiterate your main message and key points. The more they remember you, the more they'll pay attention to what you say. And that tends to help improve their memory about what you're selling!

d. **Customize your future sales.** Refer back to your notes before your next attempt to sell each customer. Refreshing your own memory about their needs and preferences will help you better position yourself to make the next big sale.

SALES TAKEAWAY

Own every Sales conversation, and assume responsibility as the chief communications person. When you guide the prospect through every interaction, you'll end up with far more sales and stronger relationships for long-term success.

6

QUIT

ASSUMING CUSTOMERS CAN SELL YOUR IDEAS TO OTHER DECISION-MAKERS.

———————

The days of the single decision-maker are long gone. Today it's rare to find situations in which one person has the full authority to review the information, make the choice, and sign the contract. We've found it's much more common to sell to "the committee," as we call it. Which means the Sales process is astronomically more complex. We're constantly selling – not just to our main contact but to an array of people we may not even get to meet.

Here's an example. In our industry, event planners might call us to inquire about keynotes on topics related to strategic Sales. They tell us they want 90 minutes of presentation time, with as much information packed in as humanly possible. Based on that, we might spend all of our energy selling the value of our content. However, we'd still lose the job.

Why? Because the people on the committee making the final decision have different ideas. Some want entertainment. Some want motivation, while others think interactive format is the top priority. Selling to achieve consensus requires a vastly different approach.

What does that mean in terms of closing the deal? We can't assume the opinions of our contact person align with everyone else on the committee. It doesn't matter if we communicate flawlessly and make a brilliant case for our products and services with our contact. What happens next is out of our hands.

It's like a relay race, and we've been forced to hand off the baton to people who aren't even on our team. We have no control over the quality of information they will deliver to the rest of the committee. No clue whether they have any Sales experience. No idea whether they will emphasize the main point or leave out some key details.

For that reason, we've learned the importance of spending quality time "teaching" our contacts how to sell the solutions we offer and the advantages of using us as suppliers. That means anticipating that the rest of the team may have different needs. It's critical to ask about those differences and proactively sell to *everyone* who is part of the process — not just the person sitting in front of us.

SALES TAKEAWAY

Find out how many people will have input into the decision to buy from you. Spend time learning about their preferences and priorities, and give your contact all the right tools to best share your solution with the group.

7

QUIT

ASSUMING PROSPECTS ARE NOT WILLING TO CHANGE.

Rarely does anyone start the morning with a bold affirmation that says, *"Please let there be tons of change today. The more the better. Bring it on. It's just what I need!"*

Nope. Change is hard. People avoid it whenever possible. So we might intuitively assume that clients don't WANT to change whatever they are doing or buying, but that doesn't mean they aren't WILLING to change. Those are two different concepts. Your job as a salesperson is to turn their dread of change into a willingness to look at the options you're presenting.

Deep down, clients recognize that change is necessary if they want to create growth for the company, increase satisfaction for their own customers, and build revenue. They can't stay right where they are and remain competitive.

On the other hand, that realization doesn't always propel them to action. Change often involves some hard work, an outlay of money, and perhaps time spent training. None of which are high in the "fun" category. So, while they may be perfectly aware of the need to move forward, sometimes it's easier to whine about it. To procrastinate. To make YOU the bad guy for trying to sell them on something new. Don't take it personally.

From that perspective, you're not really selling products or services. You're selling *change*. We both make frequent presentations on this topic, and it is an enduring truth. Without the ability to sell change, a salesperson is doomed.

Think about that. Sales is all about reworking, reorganizing, reassessing, redirecting, and reimagining. When you can sell all of that juicy potential against a backdrop of excitement rather than fear, your success will skyrocket.

Here's a tip: Don't gloss over how much work it might take temporarily to make a change. Be realistic while emphasizing the long-term benefits. Then let them know you'll be right there, every step of the way, to help lead them through the process.

SALES TAKEAWAY

Stop reacting when customers complain about change. Listen, sympathize, and move ahead with the sale. It's just what people do when they know something will involve time, effort, and money. Look beyond the griping, and help them find a solution that generates real enthusiasm. With your help, they'll see that change is worth it.

8

QUIT

ASSUMING YOU'RE EXEMPT FROM DOING THE BORING TASKS.

If you're like most salespeople, you love the thrill of the hunt. The energizing chase to find the perfect prospect. The intriguing challenge of negotiating the deal. The adrenalin buzz of getting it closed. And then...

Nothing kills a good Sales "high" like having to do all the boring work that slows you down. The time eventually comes when you have to enter details into your CRM system, write up contracts, or fill out Sales reports. Yawn.

Let's face it. These are probably the last things you want to be doing. After all, you assume those tasks are taking away from your time allotted to make more sales, right? Certainly less fun.

Point taken. However, while administrative functions aren't the most exciting part of your Sales job, they really do add value. They ensure that the prosperously fulfilling parts of your days happen as effectively and efficiently as possible. And in Sales, that's the name of the game.

Change your mindset. Instead of approaching these tasks as necessary evils like death and taxes, acknowledge the serious value they add. When you attend meetings, forecast sales, build prospecting lists, and update your customer files, you're taking steps to become a more profitable salesperson. Those things matter.

Even great race car drivers have to stop for gas. The "boring stuff" gives you the fuel you need to keep selling at top speed.

On the other hand, don't assume that every dull administrative hassle has to continue in its same form. Thankfully, advances in technology can give you a huge boost in streamlining these tasks.

Today there are dozens of Sales enablement tools with online support to help you work faster and get you back out on the trail. New options are constantly being launched. Many of them are wildly efficient and remarkably innovative.

Watch for introductions of new productivity tools for the Sales industry. Invest the time to learn about them. Perhaps try them. You never know when an amazing new process might come along, creating an administrative shortcut that saves you time *and* money.

SALES TAKEAWAY

Think about the "boring" parts of your Sales job as creating a foundation to support and enhance the part of the job you love most — selling! You can't have one without the other.

9

QUIT

ASSUMING YOU HAVE TO COLD CALL.

Go for it. Shout out all the reasons why you disagree with that statement and why you think cold calling is a great strategy. We'll wait.

First of all, here's the disclaimer. Cold calling *can* work…when it's highly targeted and appropriate for your industry. If you're using that method and it's working for you, by all means, do it! Just don't make that your primary, leading-edge strategy for finding new prospects.

In our vast Sales experience, cold calling is often the least effective way for salespeople to use their precious time and resources to close more deals. In fact, a study from the Keller Research Center at Baylor University found that *less than* 1% of cold calls actually result in a face-to-face meeting. The old Sales adage about playing the "numbers game" is simply outdated.

Today, the Sales landscape is totally different. Which, in turn, has totally changed buyer behavior. Customers can go online to find products, prices, and demonstration videos without ever talking to a salesperson. Plus, caller ID gives customers a sleek way of screening calls and ignoring anyone they don't already know. If you think it's a challenge for cold callers to get a foot in the door, imagine how hard it is when they can't even make it to the front porch.

So if cold calling isn't effective and causes most salespeople a significant amount of anxiety, why do they still feel like it's an industry requirement? The "supposed" wisdom behind cold calling is that people who don't know you will be willing to call you back, agree to see you, and buy your product. Just think about that. How often do you pick up the phone for a number you don't even recognize and then put everything aside while you listen to a scripted pitch for a product you may not even need?

Explained that way, cold calling sounds unproductive, at best. Maybe even a little crazy. Quit assuming you have to make cold calls if you want to succeed in Sales.

The best Sales strategy is to have *several* Sales strategies. Call on existing customers. Ask for referrals. Partner with other Sales reps. Network whenever you can. And yes, throw in a little cold calling if you want! Just remember that relationships matter in the world of Sales. They really matter. Customers aren't buying your product or your service; they are purchasing the opportunity to work with YOU.

SALES TAKEAWAY

Diversify your Sales strategy, and don't put all your eggs in the cold-calling basket. Spread out your resources, and invest in your prospects before you ask them to invest in you.

10

QUIT

ASSUMING ONLY
EXTROVERTS CAN SELL.

People often make the assumption that Sales is a career choice reserved for those with the "gift of gab" or that bubbly charisma that always makes them the center of attention.

News flash: Successful salespeople can be extroverts, introverts, or anything in between. They simply need to know how to use their natural gifts wisely and acquire the others through training and practice. To believe otherwise is a destructive mindset.

Let's break that down. Extroverts might think that a career in Sales is an obvious fit for their outgoing personalities. Unfortunately, assuming they were "born to sell" can sometimes make them less open to guidance. We've found that extroverts actually require the most coaching and counseling because of certain tendencies that can get in the way:

a. Talking too much and overwhelming the customers.
b. Not listening and never hearing what the customers want or need.
c. Interrupting and not letting customers finish their sentences.
d. Getting too close and being too friendly.

    e. Becoming easily distracted.

    f. Forgetting to uncover how customers want to be sold.

    g. Arguing that their solutions are better than what the customers say they want.

    h. Overselling and losing the deal.

Introverts, on the other hand, may start with an initial disadvantage. They have to work hard to develop new skills and behaviors for interpersonal communications. But once they get the hang of it, they learn and adapt in amazing ways — and they rarely take those acquired talents for granted.

When building customer relationships, there's a significant advantage to being a patient, focused listener. That might be easier for introverts, but it's also a habit that extroverts can adopt with practice.

Great salespeople can have all types of personalities, but they share a commitment to expanding their natural talents and learning new skills as they work toward their goals. Just because you're not an extrovert doesn't mean you can't be wildly successful at building relationships and meeting — or exceeding — Sales goals.

SALES TAKEAWAY

Identify whether you're an introvert or extrovert. Be authentic, but explore specific ways to leverage your strengths and minimize your weaknesses to maximize your Sales success.

11

QUIT

ASSUMING EVERYONE IS A POTENTIAL BUYER.

When we ask salespeople about their keys to success, one typical statement stops us in our tracks: *"I can sell to anybody. And I just don't take NO for an answer."* Hmmmm… Make no mistake, we admire hard work and perseverance. Stick-to-it-iveness is an asset. All day long. But for people to make the assumption that they can (and will!) sell to every person who has a pulse and some cash is just self-defeating. (Not to mention endlessly frustrating for the prospect who simply isn't interested!)

So how do you know when to keep trying and when to back down? If you follow our strategies, your assumption-free Sales process will go something like this. You'll refuse to believe your prospects aren't in a position to buy. You'll move past the fear that they aren't open to change. You'll let go of the idea they will never leave their current vendors. You'll communicate persuasively. And you'll build trust.

But if you do all of those things and the answer is still NO, it's time to stop. Pull back. By graciously accepting defeat, you can preserve the relationship, along with the glimmer of hope that someday they might need whatever you are selling.

The truth is, your goal is NOT to sell to everyone. Your success isn't determined by the quantity of your prospects, but by the *quality*. Whether they buy. How much. And how often. That underscores the enormous significance of *prequalifying leads*. Narrowing down the options. Reducing the prospect list. Deliberately choosing LESS.

We also understand the dissonance that can create. Especially in a world that values more retweets, more "likes" on Facebook, and more followers on Instagram. But when you shift into Sales mode, it's critical to remind yourself that *more* isn't necessarily better.

Sales requires a huge investment of effort, and you have a limited amount of time. Be selective. By pursuing prospects who have absolutely no need for your product or service, you're wasting time. Yours and theirs. The Sales conversation indicates whether you're the right fit for the customer — and if they're right for you. Narrowing your scope ensures that you sell from a place of power and gives you control over whom you choose to do business with.

So if you detect that a potential client simply isn't in your wheelhouse under any circumstances, move on. Invest your time with a lead that will really matter.

SALES TAKEAWAY

Examine your Sales pipeline to determine whether you are generating *quality* leads. If the prospects aren't a good fit, stop making excuses and move on to find buyers who actually need the solutions you offer.

SALES TRAITS...
THAT
ANNOY
EVERYONE

You know that salesperson who drives customers absolutely crazy? Make sure it's never YOU.

1

QUIT
TRYING TO BEFRIEND
YOUR CUSTOMERS.

———————

The capacity to build solid, healthy rapport with clients is definitely a critical trait for those in Sales. However, some salespeople lose track of their boundaries. Instead of working to create trusted business relationships, they mistakenly try to turn their clients into friends.

Is that such a bad thing, you might ask? Aren't clients more likely to do business with their friends? The answer may surprise you.

Here are a few reasons why you should avoid transforming customer relationships into friendships:

a. **We can't be completely objective with our friends.** Psychologically speaking, a friendship is an emotional attachment that has its ups and downs. We run the risk of becoming too deeply entangled in their issues, which could impact our judgment. A certain level of detachment can give us the objectivity to step aside and offer them the most appropriate solutions.

b. **We usually share too much private information with our friends.** Our customers should never get bogged down by the drama of our own personal lives. Oversharing can quickly make things awkward in business relationships, and it definitely puts us at a disadvantage as we try to promote new products and services.

c. **We lose the edge when negotiating with our friends.** To avoid the impression of pushing too hard or taking advantage of them, we may back away from trying to upsell or expand the contract. And when customers are close enough to know our strengths and weaknesses, they may use that in negotiations to their own advantage (even unintentionally).

d. **We tend to take our friends (and family) for granted.** Sad, but true. When we get used to having others around, we begin to expect certain behaviors of them – regardless of whether we are reciprocating or not. Personally and professionally, this is a sure-fire way to guarantee a relationship disaster. And in Sales, it's a loud invitation for your competitors to show up and shower these customers with the attention they aren't getting from you.

SALES TAKEAWAY

Stay focused on building healthy business relationships and maintaining your professional boundaries. If you start to confuse clients and friends, you could be sabotaging your own sales.

2

QUIT
LACKING SELF-AWARENESS.

It's an unavoidable fact. Brilliant Sales strategies are worthless if the salesperson is annoying, abrupt, or off-putting. Ouch.

When it comes to Sales, a healthy amount of self-awareness (or mindfulness) is just as important as your product and your pitch. Not an optional "soft" trait. It's essential to understand who you are, how your emotions affect your actions, and how to detach from your behaviors to pursue opportunities for self-improvement. If you don't start with an objective view of yourself, it's virtually impossible to develop strong relationships with customers.

As we train and coach salespeople, we often notice a disparity between how they describe their Sales techniques and how they actually approach their customers. The way they rank their values and beliefs frequently doesn't match up with their real-life choices, attitudes, and behaviors. In other words, there's a total disconnect between *what they do* and *what they think they do*. That disconnect signals a lack of self-awareness.

If you know someone who suffers from that type of misalignment, you know how irritating it can be. But here's the kicker. Lack of self-awareness is a deal-breaking, relationship-ruining, instant dead-end for people in Sales. It can seriously derail your career like nothing else. So before you write this off as some kind of optional self-help exercise, understand this proven principle: Enhancing your self-awareness will directly impact your ability to increase sales. No question about it.

If you might be suffering from this disconnect, here are a few ways to help boost your self-awareness:

a. **Focus on being aligned.** Pay close attention to your internal thoughts and your emotions. Compare those with the way you actually behave. Are they congruent? Are you getting the responses and reactions you expect? If not, it's time for some honest self-reflection and a commitment to change.

b. **Deliberately manage your emotions.** If you want to develop long-term relationships, engage with your customers in a way that makes them WANT to work with you. Be more sensitive to how you're coming across, and try to build rapport. When you learn to control your emotions more effectively, you'll create better results.

c. **Take an honest look back at past Sales performance.** Analyze the deals you won, the deals you lost, and the reasons why. The best way to become more self-aware is to understand exactly what's working for you and what isn't.

SALES TAKEAWAY

Balance your view of who you are as a person AND a salesperson. Be confident, but recognize areas for improvement. Make sure what you do on the outside reflects what you are thinking inside.

3
QUIT
FOCUSING ON YOUR WEAKNESSES.

The self-help industry in the U.S. is valued at more than $11 billion per year. No wonder people stay focused on their "weaknesses." But in the realm of Sales, that's simply not a helpful mind-set. Confidence and poise can be quickly diluted by feelings of inadequacy and low self-esteem.

No, we aren't discounting the importance of making improvements. Not at all. Everyone has some sort of flaw, imperfection, or disadvantage. Those don't make people weak; they make them human. Most successful people have some sort of glaring shortcoming that they've managed to overcome on their way to fame and fortune.

Thriving salespeople have learned to reframe their weaknesses as "manageable limitations" rather than "insurmountable disasters." They give themselves permission to pursue excellence in a healthy way, but they don't waste time beating themselves up for falling short of perfection. That's just counterproductive on every level.

To help you harness the power of your strengths for Sales success, try following these steps.

a. **Be honest about your own capabilities.** Nobody's perfect. Get candid about what you do well and what could use some improvement. Did we mention that nobody's perfect?

b. **Leverage your strengths.** Find more opportunities to do what you truly love. To do what you were really born to do. In Sales, you might feel completely "in your element" when sharing ideas. Negotiating. Connecting with people. Closing the deal. Whatever it is, build on that. Search for ways to increase the time you spend doing the things that showcase your greatest strengths.

c. **Develop skills that will help you reach your goals.** Your talents and strengths can't stand alone. Great skills can turn a mediocre strength into a major contender. Invest the time to build the skills that will create a foundation for your continued growth. For us, speaking might be one of our greatest strengths, but we also spend time building other profit-making skills that help expand our businesses. Branch out a little; it's the equivalent of becoming a well-rounded student.

d. **Overcome your limitations.** Figure out what's getting in the way of leveraging your strengths. If it's something you *can* change, make it happen. If it's something you *can't* change, accept it. Find an alternative. A work-around. A different solution. The only limitation to your success is allowing a perceived weakness to hold you back.

SALES TAKEAWAY

Stop obsessing about your shortcomings, and start concentrating on your strengths. That's the best way to turn your limitations into abilities (rather than liabilities).

QUIT
BEING LATE.

Traffic was terrible. I got lost. There was a long line at Starbucks. Nope. All of those answers are incorrect. Being late for a Sales call is totally unacceptable. Period. When you can't show up on time, you're basically showing the customer what it will be like to work with you. And that glimpse into the future is less than appealing. There's no excuse for being tardy to make a sale.

We don't say that to be difficult, judgmental, or tough. We say that because it's true. No matter what the reason, if you're late for a Sales call (face-to-face, phone, Skype, Webex), the potential customer will likely view whatever you have to say through the lens of doubt. You've probably blown the deal.

What's up with that? Let's look at it from the psychological standpoint. You show up late, and potential buyers could take away these harsh messages:

You're disrespectful. Apparently you don't value my time. I'm insulted. Why should I listen to your proposition when I'm already offended by your behavior?

You're selfish. You seem to think you are more important than me. Your schedule takes priority. Do I really want to build a business relationship with someone like that? Hard pass.

You're irresponsible. You approached me. You made the appointment. And yet you don't have the courtesy to show up on time. How could I ever trust you to deliver my products in a timely manner?

You're overcommitted. You seem to have too much on your plate. If you can't manage your schedule now, how could you possibly devote enough time to take care of my account?

You're uninterested. You don't appear to seriously want my business. If my account really mattered, you would arrive on time. Prepared. Enthusiastic. Do you have better things to do?

Intense, right? OK, truth be told, some people have different tolerances for tardiness. To some, five minutes isn't a big deal. They might even show up late themselves. But why risk the potential for a huge sale by assuming the buyer won't care? Don't do it.

Unless there's a natural disaster or you've experienced bodily harm, there's really no excuse to be late. Plan ahead to show that you value your customers' time. Consult your GPS. Make coffee at home. Whatever it takes. Just be punctual. End of story.

SALES TAKEAWAY

Show up on time. In Sales, your punctuality (or lack of it) tells your customers everything they need to know about doing business with you before you ever say the first word.

5

QUIT

MIRRORING YOUR CUSTOMERS.

Chances are, you've read some articles on the psychological research about "mirroring." This behavior – the ability to mimic another person's vocal tones, distance, eye contact, posture, and body language – is often described as a communication tool to help gain trust.

On one hand, if used properly and effectively, mirroring can have a positive impact. On the other hand, mirroring involves some risk. Without the right training, the right personalities, and the right situation, it can definitely backfire. And when mirroring is used inappropriately, it can create disastrous effects.

Let's unpack that. There are actually two types of mirroring: conscious and unconscious. If you're married or have been in a long-term relationship, you've no doubt experienced unconscious mirroring at its deepest level – automatically adopting some of their gestures, habits, and expressions. It's natural and normal, but it can still become grating to another person if used too often.

In Sales, people sometimes opt for conscious mirroring – purposefully mimicking customers for the sole purpose of gaining respect and trust to sell a product. First, that's a bit creepy. Second, it can totally work against you if customers recognize what you're doing. They may assume you're making fun of them. In fact, overt mirroring can be perceived as phony or patronizing. Even an insult. Not a great way to make a good impression.

So when does intentional mirroring work? In our experience, very rarely. The one mirroring technique that does provide value is recognizing a customer's speech volume and pace. Not matching it; just noticing it and using it as a guide.

If you are normally loud and dramatic, dial it back a little when you meet with a soft-spoken client. If your shy, quiet demeanor seems to be getting lost in the conversation with a boisterous prospect, be deliberate about elevating your energy level.

When you're confident about building a relationship with buyers, you'll automatically be sensitive to their preferred conversational styles. Your vocal tone and pace will follow suit, giving them the best chance to hear what you're saying.

According to the thousands of salespeople we work with, the message is clear. The best way to sell is, generally, to be yourself.

SALES TAKEAWAY

Be authentic to build stronger relationships with your prospects, while tempering any traits that could potentially be off-putting. You can sell to your customers' personalities without mirroring them.

QUIT
BEING PUSHY.

In our presentations, we often talk about the difference between being assertive and being aggressive. That's a very important distinction when it comes to Sales. Assertive salespeople are open, honest, respectful, and trustworthy. On the other hand, aggressive salespeople are arrogant, argumentative, and manipulative.

Which approach do you think will close more deals and develop more long-term relationships? Yep. Being assertive is the one and only, go-to style of interaction you should ever adopt.

Despite that obvious wisdom, people who readily employ pressure tactics and pushy strategies can still be found in every business and industry. And they inevitably fail. (Psssst…you don't want to be one of them.)

Use these techniques to make sure your Sales savvy isn't venturing into high-pressure territory:

a. **Don't confuse assertive persistence with aggressive pushiness.** Should you follow up, provide added value, and offer additional solutions? Of course! But if you're pursuing a prospect who has clearly said NO to your product, to your price or to you, let it go. If you can do that in a respectful way, you're leaving the door open for future sales.

b. **Don't argue with customers when they are trying to say no.** That's aggressive. The assertive route is to graciously ask if they'd like additional information or perhaps a chance to talk with a current client who is happy with your product or service.

c. **Don't use pressure language.** Telling customers what they MUST do, HAVE to do, or SHOULD do is unnecessarily aggressive. And it sounds bossy! Instead, use assertive phrases like, *"A great idea for you might be…"* or *"Here's a solution some of my other clients have found helpful."*

d. **Don't get into a power struggle.** If you continually interrupt your clients or correct them, you may transform a standard business negotiation into a prickly test of wills. Not exactly the environment to gain trust and loyalty. Truly listen to the customer's needs and respond without getting defensive.

e. **Don't focus on the upsell before you've even closed the deal.** Nothing puts a client in the frame of mind NOT to buy like bombarding them with options and add-ons before they've even had a chance to consider whether they need the initial product.

SALES TAKEAWAY

Choose assertive communication as the go-to choice for every Sales interaction. Aggressive, domineering tactics will push them away. And that's completely counterproductive.

7

QUIT

NEGLECTING TO PREPARE
FOR DIFFICULT CHALLENGES.

Remember those rare geniuses in school who could just show up and ace every test without studying? We often encounter salespeople who believe they, too, are exempt from the hard work that comes before success. Shouldn't their natural charisma, sparkling personalities, and advanced conversational skills make up for a moderate level of product knowledge?

No! A million times, no! They may have elevated themselves to a place where they think they can "wing it" with their Sales process, but that's simply not true. Not if they want to advance their Sales careers to the next level.

Why? Today's buyers demand more. They're well informed, fully in control, and often skeptical. They can dig up virtually any information they need online, so they don't have to settle for someone who offers charm without substance. They deserve a salesperson who understands their businesses. Someone who can share innovative insights. Add serious value. And answer difficult questions.

If you want to be that kind of salesperson, you've got to be prepared. Ready for the usual drill, but also for the unexpected.

We're talking about the questions, the objections, and the challenges you didn't see coming. In this competitive landscape, you can bet that clients are going to push back on whatever you're selling. On the price. On the quality. On the timing. And sooner or later, you're going to be faced with potential customers who are nitpicky fault-finders in search of a heated debate.

To combat that kind of scrutiny, salespeople have to "know their stuff." Backward and forward. Upside down. They need a solid understanding of the industry — how it's evolved and where it's headed. Then they need to examine their products at a microscopic level to uncover every potential problem, flaw, and imperfection that could possibly be questioned by an interested prospect. In response, they have to gather the research to prove why their product is still the best option.

One more thing. Preparation has another facet that is often overlooked. Practice eliminating any traces of an argumentative tone. You have to learn how to counter objections and provide your rationale without sounding angry or defensive. When you can enter negotiations fully informed and ready to handle unexpected questions in a collaborative way, you'll be prepared to build credibility and trust that can seal the deal.

SALES TAKEAWAY

Set yourself up for Sales success by doing your research. Demonstrate to the customers that you aren't just there for a Sales call. You want to partner with them and invest in growing their business.

8

QUIT

USING TIRED SALES JARGON.

We may not like to admit it, but the Sales profession doesn't always have the best reputation. Some people may tend to, shall we say, be a little skeptical about the underlying motives involved.

To overcome that potentially negative perception, salespeople need to make every effort to demonstrate their authenticity. And that's exactly why they need to avoid reinforcing old, less-than-flattering stereotypes by infusing their messages with unnecessary Sales jargon and overused clichés.

Nothing shuts down a productive Sales conversation like peppering in those phrases that just scream, *"This is the same, boring speech I give at every appointment."* You know exactly what we're talking about: *"We are customer-focused. We give 110% every day. Our products are best-in-class. We provide turnkey service. This is a great opportunity for you."*

Honestly, that type of language prompts an Olympic-level eye roll from virtually everyone. Including us. *Especially us.*

You can find ways to express those basic sentiments without throwing in canned, robotic statements that land with a deafening thud. Talk about a guaranteed deal-killer! Skip the sentences you think customers want to hear or whatever jargon you learned in an outdated training course. Let go of the idea that you must use the "magic Sales phrases" that will resonate with customers and seal the deal every time. Those don't exist. (We would tell you if they did. We promise!)

Just stop talking. Instead, ask open-ended questions. Listen to the answers. Allow the conversation to flow. Focus on the customer's needs and how you can add value to the relationship. Find a more authentic and organic way to deliver your messages. That's the very best way to break out of the dull, Sales-script habit. And, as a bonus, you just might help to make a positive change in the way people view the industry. Sweet!

SALES TAKEAWAY

Skip the jargon that alienates potential customers, and focus on authentically doing what you do best – connecting with them and providing solutions that will help them grow their businesses.

9

QUIT
CONFUSING CONFIDENCE AND ARROGANCE.

Most people would agree that a career in Sales requires confidence. But after that, things aren't quite as clear-cut. Contrary to popular belief, confidence is not measured on a sliding scale. This line of faulty thinking says lack of confidence makes you a doormat, while overly high confidence makes you arrogant. From that angle, the "perfect" level of confidence must be somewhere in between. Psychologically speaking, that's just NOT how it works.

The traits of confidence and arrogance aren't on the same continuum at all. Not even close. Confidence is based on positivity, trust, reality, and respect. Arrogance is based on status, braggadocio, superiority, and control. To believe arrogance is just an overabundance of confidence is an unfortunate misunderstanding. And a tragic myth.

If you're in Sales, it's critical to recognize how confidence affects your ability to sell. It's like the air you breathe; you've got to have it. To nurture it. To protect it. Because without it, you're basically inviting arrogance to swoop in and take over.

So what do we know about confidence? Sometimes it helps to define *what it is* by looking at *what it isn't*.

a. **Confidence doesn't come with a rule book.** It's different for every person. The trick is to figure out what it looks like for you in your role as a salesperson.

b. **Confidence isn't something you can fake.** It's an inside job. So just acting confident will get you into trouble every time. When you genuinely have confidence, it shows. When you don't, arrogance makes a grand entrance. And arrogance doesn't sell.

c. **Confidence doesn't apply to bullies.** People who use put-downs and humiliation to gain power over others are NOT confident. When salespeople try to steam-roll over clients and force them to buy products they don't need, that's the result of pure arrogance.

d. **Confidence isn't disrespectful.** A huge part of being confident is the ability to be courteous and deferential. To respect others. To hear feedback without getting defensive. Arrogant salespeople argue and lecture condescendingly.

e. **Confidence doesn't guarantee you'll always be the winner.** Confident salespeople recognize that there may be others who can sell more, recruit more, and rise to the top faster than they do. They're comfortable with that. Arrogant salespeople pretend to be more powerful than they really are and exude a sense of entitlement. Customers can see right through that every time.

SALES TAKEAWAY

Make sure your Sales persona is rooted in confidence rather than arrogance. Watch for the tell-tale signs. If you argue, interrupt or get defensive, arrogance might be undermining your Sales success.

10

QUIT

ASKING IRRELEVANT QUESTIONS.

Patient college professors often try to calm the nerves of anxious students by telling them, *"There's no such thing as a bad question."* Unfortunately, that doesn't hold true in the world of Sales. Sorry.

Any question that immediately perturbs or irritates a potential buyer is NOT a good question. That typically happens when people inquire about something that is irrelevant to the conversation or a blatant time-waster (requesting an answer the customer knows you already have or one you SHOULD have if you'd done your homework). Don't do it. And if your question might in any way be perceived as insulting, manipulating or patronizing, don't ask it. Tough love.

During our years of coaching and speaking to Sales professionals around the world, we've compiled a list of the WORST questions asked during a Sales pitch:

a. **What can you tell me about your business?** That's just unnecessary. Visit the website. Search online for company history and backstory. You can always ask for additional details, but don't expect them to start at the beginning.

b. **Are you the decision-maker?** This is verging on offensive. It's like saying, *"Are you important enough for me to be* *talking to you?"* A better choice is asking, *"Are there others I should include when sending my proposal?"*

c. **What's your budget?** That question sends the message that your price might be flexible based on the dollars they allocated. Totally misses the point of selling value over price.

d. **Who are you currently working with?** If you couldn't find that information in your preliminary research, you aren't ready for the call. Go back and do more homework.

e. **Is your current provider taking good care of you?** Irrelevant. If they are willing to talk with you, there's a fair chance the existing vendor isn't knocking it out of the park.

f. **How much are you currently paying for the product or service?** The truth is, that's none of your business. Focus on the value you can bring and the advantages you offer.

g. **What if I could save you money?** Positioning your product as the cheapest will make you vulnerable the next time your competitors offer a "special deal." Terrible strategy. Prospects need to buy from you for reasons other than price.

h. **Can I give you a second opinion?** Don't assume you are in second place. You are making a valid proposal, so position your bid with confidence as a winning solution.

i. **What will it take to get your business?** Really?! You can win the business if you provide an affordable solution to meet their needs better than the alternatives. They shouldn't have to tell you that.

SALES TAKEAWAY

Avoid asking questions that could undermine your credibility and annoy your prospects. Do your homework. Then present yourself as a knowledgeable, resourceful partner.

QUIT

MISUSING TECHNOLOGY.

From self-driving cars to drone-delivered groceries, technology can be a mind-blowing, awe-inspiring thing. It can also have a profound impact on the Sales process, although not exclusively in a positive way.

On one side, we see the traditionalists, many of whom have been in Sales for years. Even decades. They firmly see it as a "people business." Their journey toward success involves regularly connecting through face-to-face meetings, checking in with phone conversations, and attending networking events. In person. And very personal.

As you might expect, we are also seeing a new wave of Sales professionals, primarily in the younger demographics, who have fully embraced the digital approach. They like to communicate with clients through email and follow up with quick texts. They search for leads online and track the social media profiles of their prospects. It's fast. Convenient. And modern.

Which approach is better? Actually, they are both correct. There's no doubt that you can dramatically increase your efficiency by incorporating technology into your Sales process. Today's customers expect you to have an online presence that simplifies communication. Advanced CRM systems and automated outreach programs can help you to stay organized, uncover promising leads, and extend your reach.

But you also can't deny the power of human contact. The warm smiles and friendly handshakes. The ability to read the customer's body language. The chance to go off-script and uncover hidden opportunities for expanding the sale. If you want to develop and solidify a working relationship, it's hard to beat a live, one-on-one, real-time conversation.

The key is determining the proper amount of "technology" that's appropriate for communicating with each unique customer. You'll lose out if your prospects are searching online for everything they need while you're waiting to set up a meeting. The same thing happens if you're bombarding them with text messages and they really prefer to strategize in the conference room over coffee. Salespeople who misuse technology – applying too much or too little – will discover that it creates a significant barrier to their success.

SALES TAKEAWAY

Analyze the way you incorporate technology to communicate with your prospects and provide service after the sale. To maximize your effectiveness, find an approach that seamlessly combines meaningful, in-person Sales contact with efficient online strategies. Both are vitally important.

QUIT

EXAGGERATING.

At its core, Sales involves positioning a product as the superior choice compared with all of the other options available to potential customers. That's why salespeople find it so, so hard to resist the seductive lure of superlatives: This is the GREATEST product on the market. This is the FASTEST solution in the industry. This is the LOWEST price of the season. This is the HIGHEST quality you can buy. And on and on it goes.

Oh yes, superlatives have the power to make our products stand out in a big way. Like verbal spikes that help us stake a claim in the competitive landscape. But do they represent the truth? Or are they just attention-grabbing exaggerations?

We are definitely living in a world now that seems to accept exaggeration in many forms. Those intricately photoshopped images of your neighbor's blissfully happy family on Instagram may not reflect the reality of their lives — the wrinkles and extra pounds, the grumpy attitudes, the stress of maxed-out credit cards.

As you probably know, exaggeration in Sales is nothing new. From the beginning of time, Sales attracted a certain segment of people who lacked integrity and values. They manipulated unwitting customers into buying all kinds of products that could never live up to the advance hype. Or they exaggerated by omission, selectively leaving out certain facts or fine print that would certainly give the customers pause.

The good news? Things are changing. Salespeople are working hard to achieve a higher standard of behavior, and customers are beginning to hold them accountable. Exaggeration is now losing its appeal for two important reasons:

a. **Exaggeration can easily be identified today.** With the click of a mouse, customers can access online reviews and competitor websites that indicate whether you're a straight shooter or a truth stretcher. The proof is easy to find.

b. **Exaggeration erodes trust.** If salespeople make claims and promises they can't back up, their integrity will be tarnished and their relationships will disintegrate. Poof! And trust is a deal-breaker for developing loyal, long-term customers.

SALES TAKEAWAY

Believe in what you sell, and be truthful about it. Full disclosure. Overplaying your hand will always come back to bite you. And if customers feel cheated, they're likely to spread the word.

13

QUIT
BEING AN ORDER-TAKER.

In the era of Amazon, people can go online to order virtually anything and have it delivered to their doors the next day. Sometimes even the same day. So why would customers even need a salesperson who is simply a glorified order-taker? Short answer: They wouldn't.

Being an order-taker is hopelessly old school. Customers today expect much more. If they are going to invest the time to talk with a salesperson, they want someone who understands the new challenges that face their companies and their industries. They want a consultant who can help them envision new, creative solutions to the problems they are encountering.

While all of that is true, some people still choose to stay rooted in the role of order-taker. Especially if they've been selling in an industry with little to no competition. It's so easy, but also quite boring. They just sit back. Wait for the orders to be placed. Respond to any customer requests. Take the commission. Why should they make a change when that approach to Sales is almost effortless?

Oh, for so many reasons. By definition, salespeople need to embrace change. They need to drive it. Promote it. Thrive in it.

Complacency stifles their enthusiasm for change and dampens their level of selling influence. Sales professionals need to break out of the order-taker mold if they want to position themselves as agents of change who offer innovative solutions to meet customer needs.

What does that mean for you? Your customers' competitive landscapes are constantly changing and evolving, too. You have the opportunity to help them increase their sales, revenue, and market share. But if you don't take the lead to help them do that, you may become invisible. And then, when you least expect it, competitors in some form will pop up and become the champions of change your customers desperately need.

Move past the mundane task of order-taking and invest the time to influence your customers' thoughts and beliefs. Overcome their objections. Help to fuel their growth. Take on the role of consultant. Don't blend in to the background. If you're going to be in Sales, why not make it more exciting and more profitable?

SALES TAKEAWAY

Ask yourself whether you are proactively pursuing sales or just taking orders. Sales is about being one step ahead of your customers, offering them products to solve their problems before they even know they need them. If you're not adding value — sharing ideas and strategies to help them increase profits and market share BEYOND selling them products — your customers may find a competitor who will.

QUIT

OVERSELLING.

Maybe it's nerves. Maybe it's adrenalin. Maybe it's habit. But it's absolutely excruciating. We're talking about the salespeople who seem to lack the basic ability to just SHUT UP. Harsh, we know. But if this applies to you, we want this chapter to be the wake-up call you genuinely need.

In many cases, salespeople who oversell are wildly enthusiastic about their products, but they are much more focused on their own personal goals and quotas. Instead of listening to the customers' needs and concerns, these salespeople launch into a lively mono- logue of product features, examples, research, and real-world anecdotes. Sometimes they even keep on talking AFTER the deal is closed.

If that scenario sounds vaguely familiar, it's time to ask yourself the question: Are you prone to overselling? Here are three clues that might help you find the answer – and learn how to respond:

a. **Your customers begin to argue with you.** Take the hint: You've somehow overstepped. While your first inclination might be to ramp up the debate, back off and give your customers some room. Becoming combative (or being perceived that way) will never close a deal.

b. **Your customers begin to look distracted.** Pay attention to their body language. Checking phones, preparing to stand, and moving toward the door are clear signals they want out. You may have overstated your case, so force yourself to pleasantly wrap things up.

c. **Your customers shut down.** Watch for the signs. Are your customers engaged, asking questions, and responding with more than one-word answers? If not, you're overselling. Your customers may have mentally checked out.

It's also helpful to consider which factors might be prompting you to oversell. Are you worried about meeting your quota? Are you trying to build credibility by demonstrating your in-depth product knowledge? Does silence make you nervous? Identify the underlying cause, and you'll have a head start in solving the problem.

As you talk to your customers, ask strategic questions. Listen more than you talk. Make them the focal point. When you do switch to selling mode, streamline your key messages. Invite dialogue throughout the process rather than racing to the finish line by sharing every product fact you know. Think of it as a conversation, and you'll be ahead of the game.

SALES TAKEAWAY

Use your time with customers wisely. Don't overload them with information or continue pushing forward when it's clear that they have had enough. If they feel like the meeting has become a hostage situation, your chances of making the sale go down. Way, way down.

15

QUIT

BEING SWAYED BY NEGATIVE PEOPLE.

We are both constantly amazed at just how many grumpy sales-people we run into on a weekly basis. Yes, we know it's a tough job. Full of rejection. Unreturned calls. Difficult customers. Long hours. But truthfully, most people understand from the beginning that those hazards come along with the "highs" of a career in Sales. So what's behind all the poor attitudes?

In many cases, that negativity is caused by hanging out with toxic people (quite possibly those also facing the difficult challenges of Sales). Before you protest and claim that your cheery disposition makes you completely immune to that kind of discontent, let us assure you: You are not. Negativity is sneaky and insidious. Like an airborne virus you can't even see. Before you realize what happened, that crippling energy seeps in and drains you of every optimistic, encouraging thought you've ever had. Trying to sell from that kind of mindset is a perilous, uphill battle.

Our simple solution: Stay away from those negative influences. Far, far away. They will rub off on you and destroy your ability to succeed in Sales. On the surface, that might seem overly dramatic, but it's the cold, hard truth.

a. **Negative people get inside your brain.** If you spend too much time with them, you'll find yourself questioning everything that's good in the world. It's basically impossible to generate enthusiasm about your product from that dark mental valley, turning every sales pitch into the pitiful, drooping helium balloon at the birthday party.

b. **Negative people are usually sad or angry.** Reflecting those emotions at the negotiating table (or in your personal relationships) is the recipe for disaster. If your friends or co-workers constantly want you to be their therapist so they can complain about their lives, it might be time to rethink how you spend your time. And with whom you spend it.

c. **Negative people want you to be as miserable as they are.** It's true; misery loves company. You'll quickly find yourself commiserating and believing that your day was just as bad as theirs. Even worse, you'll feel like you have to downplay your own success to avoid making the people around you jealous or upset.

d. **Negative people can ruin your reputation.** Right or wrong, people will judge you by those you associate with. If you're trying to increase your sales, you may not want to be recognized as the person who always hangs out with the chronic complainers.

SALES TAKEAWAY

Remember that attitudes are infectious, so be selective about the people who surround you. If you associate with those who radiate a positive attitude and an enthusiasm for life, you'll have a much brighter future for building profitable Sales relationships.

16

QUIT
LETTING YOUR EGO DO THE TALKING.

For decades, we have been training, coaching, and speaking to high-performing salespeople who consistently lead their teams to exceed ambitious goals. The first thing we usually address with these audiences is an undeniable truth: *A big ego naturally comes with the Sales territory.* The responses to that statement range from knowing smiles to hearty laughter. Say what you want, but those big egos are producing big bucks.

On the upside, a big ego is what allows salespeople to step out of the crowd and into a spotlight. It's what gives them the drive to be the best. It's what propels them to close a deal that everyone else said couldn't be done. It can also be the thing that stops them in their tracks. Why? Those bold egos sometimes prompt our mouths to talk before our ears can listen. Bad idea.

Rest assured, we have learned our lessons about ego the hard way. Early on, trying to book prestigious speaking gigs with blue-chip clients involved much more talking than listening. When we wanted a new client that much, it was hard to resist the urge to tout every award and honor and experience that would make us perfect for the job. All at once. Without taking a breath. Overwhelming, to say the least.

On another occasion, one of us launched into a spectacular Sales pitch after a potential customer asked a single question on a preliminary phone interview: *"Are you a motivational speaker?"* Without skipping a beat, the sell was on. The prospect was enthusiastically bombarded with rich, detailed examples of prior audiences who had been inspired and energized and moved to achieve remarkable things.

It was a truly outstanding explanation…right up to the point when the customer interrupted and said, *"Wait, we definitely **don't** want a motivational speaker."* Click. Face palm.

We share those stories because we've ALL had moments like that, haven't we? It happens. But we need to learn from them. Our egos themselves aren't a bad thing. But egos that go unchecked can lead directly to lost sales.

The next time you're trying to make a sale (or just interacting with another human being), STOP. Listen first. You'll have your chance! In the meantime, think "Service" rather than "Sales." What does this person want and need from you right now? They will almost always tell you outright or give you solid clues. If you can apply that information to customize your response, the Sales part will be easy. Just deliver whatever they are asking for with professionalism and integrity.

SALES TAKEAWAY

Recognize that you don't already know everything about your prospect and what they need. Listen first, and keep your ego in check.

NEGOTIATION TACTICS...
THAT DIMINISH YOUR POWER

To close more deals, you've got to close the door on those outdated strategies that are undermining your success.

① QUIT

UNDERESTIMATING THE POWER OF NEGOTIATION.

The last thing salespeople want to do is leave money on the table. But that's exactly what happens when they fail to confidently negotiate their fees or effectively communicate their value propositions.

Granted, negotiations aren't necessarily fun. Or easy. And most people aren't born with the innate skills needed for the task. Those have to be learned and practiced. Even after decades of combined selling experience, we are both still discovering new and better ways to negotiate and consistently close deals. It's an ongoing process.

While that might sound like a hassle, the need to negotiate isn't going away. It's a serious, mandatory reality in the world of Sales. Invest the time to learn more and get comfortable with the give-and-take of attracting new customers. If you make negotiating a priority in your professional development, you can put yourself in a position of power every time you follow up on a lead.

Beyond the functional skills of negotiations, these guiding principles will help you maintain your focus on Sales success.

a. **Understand the goal.** Gather enough information to make sure you know the exact problems that your customers need to solve. Customers don't buy drills; they buy the holes the drills can make. Your negotiations will be more effective if you can sell the specific solutions they need and help them understand the value they will gain.

b. **Clarify the expectations.** Determine whether their budgets match their expectations. If they expect the Lexus but can only afford the Chevy, negotiations need to address that disparity and provide options.

c. **Think big.** Some salespeople limit themselves and their customers by not thinking big enough. Don't be afraid to present something more elaborate or more expensive than you think customers will actually go for. Show them the best solution, and plant the seed for a bigger sale next time.

d. **Be patient.** Avoid the temptation to offer quick deals and instant discounts. Outstanding negotiators pull customers up to the price rather than fall down to their budgets. And don't be afraid to give the buyer a chance to think about your proposal. Sometimes removing the pressure adds credibility to the deal.

SALES TAKEAWAY

Harness the power of negotiations, and your Sales potential will be limitless. You'll make the sales. You'll build the relationships. And you'll never leave money on the table.

2

QUIT

LOSING NEGOTIATIONS
BEFORE YOU EVER START.

For those who embark on a career in Sales, the professional development opportunities are vast. But, according to industry research, 80% of all salespeople report wanting to become better negotiators. Makes perfect sense. Without the ability to effectively and creatively negotiate more deals, this exciting and unlimited career path will turn into an abrupt dead-end.

Unfortunately, many salespeople lose negotiations before they even start by shortchanging the process. We'll cover many of these topics in greater detail, but let's begin with a handy list of negotiation steps you want to follow for every single sale.

a. **Understand the playing field.** Do the research to know what your competitors offer and how much they charge. If you discover that your prices are the highest in the industry, don't panic. You can use that to your advantage when you are selling value.

b. **Establish your goals.** Walk into the room prepared. Know what you want and know what you're willing to give up. Visualize the desired outcome.

c. **Listen first.** Let them talk before you start selling. What problems do they need solved? What are their priorities? Who are their customers? Whatever they say could change the entire direction of your negotiation.

d. **Set yourself apart.** Define the unique things you offer that no one else can.

e. **Sell value.** Keep your negotiation focused on the benefits, not the money.

f. **Be collaborative.** Don't try to argue with the customer about who's right and who's wrong. If you focus on winning the battle, you're going to lose the sale. Instead, focus on how you can BOTH win and reap rewards.

g. **Use time to your advantage.** Know their deadlines and required dates for key deliverables. If you can deliver faster than your competitors, you've got an edge.

h. **Ask for the business.** This is not the time to be vague or unassertive. Let your customers know you want to work with them.

i. **Allow for a tiny concession.** Be willing to provide some added value without compromising on price.

j. **Remain confident.** Don't give in to last-minute demands. Those are often just a test to see if the deal they got was fair.

SALES TAKEAWAY

Make it a priority to become a skilled negotiator. If you want to close deals, make money, and have a successful career in Sales, this is an area where you want to become an expert.

3

QUIT

FORGETTING TO SELL
YOURSELF FIRST.

In today's marketplace, customers can buy products anywhere. With a basic Google search, they can find a multitude of resources that would likely meet their needs. So what's the incentive for them to pick up the phone and call YOU instead of heading to one of your competitors? The answer is simple, although not necessarily easy. It's all about strengthening relationships and building trust. In other words, you have to sell YOURSELF first!

Keep in mind that customers are often uncertain about what to do. They want reassurance that they are making the right decisions. They want help navigating the information overload. They want ideas about how to get the most out of their purchases. Yes, they *need* a particular product, but they *want* someone who can help them feel good about the transaction and provide justification for their final decision to buy. Your ability to guide them through those doubts and concerns will determine whether or not you walk away with the sale.

From that perspective, customers are buying YOU first, not the product. Despite all the options for global resourcing and price comparisons, deep down they still prefer the security of having a trusted partner rather than an anonymous vendor. Position yourself to be that valued resource – the consultant they can trust and look to for solutions – and your sales will go through the roof.

To build those relationships, develop a clear and compelling personal value proposition. Be able to articulate what you bring to the table beyond your product benefits. Why should they buy from you, work with you, and trust you MORE than your competitors?

When you can communicate those unique advantages and demonstrate them, your customers will recognize that you have their best interests at heart. You have the opportunity to convince them that you're absolutely the best person to buy from – someone they can believe in, count on, turn to for advice, and trust unconditionally.

Sometimes that means recommending a solution with a less-expensive product to help them save some money. But that selfless attitude creates an unbreakable, long-term loyalty that can lead to much higher sales over time, even overcoming minor price differences or quality glitches along the way. In a world where products and pricing are barely distinguishable from one another, YOU are the one thing your competition doesn't have. Sell that first!

SALES TAKEAWAY

Remember that the strongest Sales tools you have are your one-of-a-kind, personal connections with your customers. Similar products may be available from other sources, but customers want to do business with people they know and trust. Make them want to buy from YOU!

4

QUIT

FAILING TO INTEGRATE
THEIR STORIES.

Many salespeople are natural-born storytellers. Without much prompting, they can launch into compelling recitations about the proud history of their companies. Impressive case studies from current customers. Even lengthy sagas about their own triumphs as Sales professionals. Sometimes an overabundance of enthusiasm can make all those stories come tumbling out before the customer even says a word. Perhaps it's an occupational hazard.

Here's the problem. Salespeople can get so wrapped up in telling their own stories that they forget about the most important story of all. The only one that really matters: the story of the prospect.

Instead of thinking about your Sales stories as the main feature, make the customers and their challenges the centerpiece of everything you discuss. That means the buyers always talk first. Listen closely. Absorb the details about their companies, their cultures, and their unique market situations. Let them take the lead on sharing information before you take your turn. This shift in order of speaking is certainly important, but the biggest challenge comes next.

We know that your Sales stories are probably polished and well-rehearsed. The key messages are carefully structured, and you stay on point by sticking to the script. Hang on, it's time to flip over that apple cart. Stop thinking about your stories as free-standing sound-bites that can be dropped in whenever it's your turn to talk. Everything you say after first hearing the prospects' stories should be customized to fit whatever they told you. Reorder. Reorganize. Refocus.

Yes, that's a little harder. But it's a major Sales magnet. If the customers identify the biggest problem they are facing, the lead-in to your story should be exactly how you can solve that problem. Adjust your pitch. When you dive in immediately with targeted relief for their pain points, your customers will get excited about working with you and using your products.

Demonstrate relevance. Create emotion. Ignite urgency. Position yourself as a problem-solver, not just a vendor. By customizing your Sales messages, you're providing the bridge that helps your prospects see the connection between their business and your products. *Their* story needs to be *your* story.

SALES TAKEAWAY

Discover your prospects' stories first, and allow those to become the main plot line in your Sales conversations. When you can weave your messages into their narrative, you'll likely be rewarded by successfully closing the deal.

5

QUIT

MAKING MONEY YOUR TOP PRIORITY.

———————

Some people openly admit that they chose a career in Sales because of the enormous potential for earning money. They like being in control of their own destiny. The more they hustle, the more cash ends up in their accounts. It's a beautiful equation.

As we've said before, there's absolutely nothing wrong with earning money — even great money — and enjoying it every step of the way. We recommend it. We encourage it! Money is a direct reflection of your hard work, talents, and expertise. But here's the irony.

If you want to make more money as a salesperson, stop thinking about the commission check. Your top priority needs to be your customers. Connecting with them. Educating them. Helping them. Impacting them. Providing solutions for them. The more you focus on your customers, the more successful you will be.

Concentrating on the cash throws everything off. It actually undermines Sales behaviors and negotiation styles, pushing money away rather than attracting it. When salespeople are blinded by the dollar signs, they may sabotage their own ability to meet broader expectations. They start selling price rather than solutions. And it's a real shame.

That's exactly the problem for salespeople who make money their first and only priority. We've seen it so many times. Salespeople recognize that their products aren't quite the right fit for their customers, but they still apply the hurry-up-and-close-the-deal approach.

Finding better solutions for customers might take more time — and could involve failing to meet the immediate goals — but that effort is often rewarded with exponentially bigger sales the following year and much stronger relationships. Short-term loss. Long-term gain. In a nutshell, letting the money drive the process is a Sales strategy that never wins.

When solutions are your top priority, your customers will buy in higher quantities, upgrade more often, and happily sing your praises to other potential customers. Best of all? You'll reap the benefits in dollars and cents. Customers will quickly recognize the disparity between a salesperson who is focused on meeting their needs versus someone who just wants to close the deal and grab the commission.

Be clear about your priorities. And remember that earning great money should be the RESULT of an awesome Sales career, not the main REASON for it.

SALES TAKEAWAY

Put your customers first. Make it your mission to add value for them. When your attention, purpose, agenda, motivation, and behaviors begin and end with the customer, money will have an uncanny way of finding you.

6

QUIT

FOCUSING ON THE COMPETITION.

In the Sales industry, tough competitors can drive you crazy — or they can drive you to perform at a higher level. The truth is, you can probably always find a competitor with a superior product or a cheaper price. Important information to know, for sure, but it shouldn't be your primary focus. And if it is, you've got a problem.

Entering Sales negotiations with a pervasive fear that someone else can offer better quality or a lower cost will automatically put you at a disadvantage. You might become so hyper-focused on the strengths of the competitive products that you become blind to their weaknesses. And those weaknesses are exactly what help you define your own competitive advantage.

Yes, you need to do your homework and know what you're up against. That will give you the information you need to create an appropriate strategy. How does your product stack up to the alternatives? How do the prices compare? As we have said over and over again, customers are usually willing to pay more once you convince them that the value they receive will be worth every penny and help to grow their businesses.

Once you know the basic comparisons, turn your full attention back to the products or services you want them to buy from YOU. Spend your time positioning your product to meet the specific customer needs your competitors don't. Find ways to outshine and outperform them from multiple angles.

What your competitors do (or don't do) is outside of your control. You can't make them lower their prices, lower their quality, or lower their standards. The only thing you can control is how you sell your value as the heart and soul of your negotiations.

To succeed, keep your own products at the forefront. Make your competitors a reference point, not the focal point. Finding a healthy balance between those two will give you the perspective you need to sell more effectively and more successfully.

SALES TAKEAWAY

Be knowledgeable about your competitors, but invest more of your time in finding ways to sell the distinct value of your products and the solutions they can provide for your customers. Understand your competitors, just don't over-emphasize them.

7

QUIT
GIVING AWAY CONTROL
OF THE CONVERSATION.

If you want to control the sale, you've got to control the conversation! When we coach and train salespeople, we often discover that this is a frequently overlooked Sales strategy.

Understandably, you've got a lot on your mind when you head into a Sales call. Topics to cover. Goals to achieve. But without a conversation plan, it's tough to keep the meeting on track. And once you lose control of the meeting, you're likely to lose the sale.

Here's how it happens. Prospects might get sidetracked complaining about internal politics and employee drama unrelated to the products you're trying to sell. Or the prospects might launch into a diatribe about the stock market, current events, technology or whatever's on their minds — not in a "getting to know you and building relationships" way, but in a "rambling off topic and totally wasting my time" way. Suddenly they announce they have another appointment, and your unproductive meeting is over.

In all of these situations, the salespeople have completely given up control of the conversation. They desperately need to get back into the driver's seat! If this tends to happen to you, these tips could help return the steering wheel to your capable hands.

a. **Demonstrate that you're in charge.** Set the stage right from the beginning that you've done your homework and you're prepared for the call. Take the lead quickly and succinctly. Then sit back and listen.

b. **Go in with a plan.** Have a defined strategy for how you want the Sales call to go. Expect the conversation to wander on occasion, but have some pre-determined tactics to help you get back on track.

c. **Dive in and ask smart, pertinent questions.** Get to the heart of what you need to know to really add value to the relationship and differentiate yourself from your competition. Just don't drone on and on with your questions. And definitely don't become so aggressive that your potential buyers start to feel like they are in an FBI interrogation.

d. **Guide the sale to a close.** Describe the positive impact they'll enjoy by using your products. Ask for the business. If they need to discuss your options with a committee, nail down the timing of your next conversation. Take charge of the follow-up contact, and set another meeting or call before you leave the office.

SALES TAKEAWAY

Position yourself in a place of power during a Sales conversation rather than a place of desperation. Develop and implement a specific plan to set the tone for the meeting, gather information, present your ideas, and make firm plans for the next steps. But don't forget that silence and active listening are also powerful tools.

8

QUIT

FAILING TO ASK TOUGH QUESTIONS.

When customers have challenging questions during negotiations, GOOD salespeople are fully prepared to answer. But GREAT salespeople are ready with tough questions of their own.

We can always tell the quality of salespeople by the quality of the questions they ask. Do they ask basic questions they could really answer on their own with a glance at the website? Or do they have the courage to ask deeper questions that challenge the thinking of their potential buyers – maybe even pushing them out of their comfort zones? Deeper questions create a far stronger and more powerful Sales conversation.

"What changes do you have planned when the new compliance regulations take effect next year?" "Have you considered shifting the way you bundle your products in light of your new competitive pressures?" "Could you perhaps automate that process to save time and money?"

Hard questions help our prospects think about their current situations in a completely different way. These questions may open buyers up to new ideas and better results. And, last but not least, these questions show that we're willing to leverage our own brain power to explore potential solutions for their problems. We're consultants. Partners.

Considering those positive outcomes, why would salespeople NOT want to ask hard questions? The short answer is fear. Fear of making prospects angry. Fear of looking ignorant. But not asking hard questions means losing out on the chance to create game-winning, career-making, long-lasting relationships. To increase your comfort level with asking hard questions, what things do you need?

a. **Trust.** Build a connection with your prospects, and invest in the relationships first. If they trust you, they will open up to you and listen to your opinions. Even respect them.

b. **Knowledge.** Understand your prospects and their industries. If you are going to push a customer in a new direction, you need to really know what you're talking about.

c. **Courage.** No sugar-coating this one: It takes guts. Asking hard questions isn't easy, and you have to be prepared for your customers to push back. Trust us, they will.

d. **Persistence.** Don't give up if your buyers initially resist. It may take more than one tough question to help them understand your perspective or the bigger issues at play. Just make sure your positive intent is reflected in your respectful tone.

SALES TAKEAWAY

Commit to being prepared and supporting your customers with broader thinking that may prompt some difficult questions. And when you ask, you're proving that you have what it takes to add real value to your customer relationships.

9

QUIT

WRITING UNIMAGINATIVE PROPOSALS.

———

You knocked the Sales conversation out of the park. You connected with the prospect. Everything was going well – until you sent over the proposal. It was too long, too disorganized, and too confusing. A major misstep.

Don't let an unimaginative proposal ruin a great opportunity. A Sales proposal should be simple to read, easy to understand, and perfectly clear. But it should also stand out as personalized, creative, and memorable. Sometimes even fun! Beyond that, customers should quickly be able to consume the information in the proposal and pinpoint exactly what you are asking them to buy or do.

From a broader view, the key to developing an effective Sales proposal is thinking about every component from the customers' perspectives. What do they really care about? What is most important to them? Why does your product or solution matter? In what ways can you help them achieve their goals? Information that veers off topic from those parameters will become worthless in a proposal. Even worse, that extraneous data could overwhelm your prospect and derail your opportunity to close the sale.

Follow these guidelines to create a powerful Sales proposal that gets results.

a. **Short and content-driven.** Concise is always better. Make it easy to read and understand so that deciphering it isn't a painful chore.

b. **Customized.** With one glance, prospects can detect a cookie-cutter proposal – something off-the-shelf with the company name dropped in. The point is to demonstrate how much you understand about their unique businesses and their needs. And that should be the featured content in a specific, customized proposal.

c. **Well-written and proofread.** Your English teacher wasn't exaggerating: Grammar, punctuation and spelling are critical. If you don't show attention to detail on the proposal, why should the buyers trust you to be detail-oriented in servicing their accounts? Solid sentence structure and a logical flow of ideas will keep them interested and engaged as they read.

d. **Solution-focused.** The most important part of any proposal is showcasing the benefits for your prospects. What's in it for them? Highlight the ways you can improve results, increase efficiencies, or just make their lives better.

SALES TAKEAWAY

Create proposals that are customized to the potential buyer's specific needs. Keep them short, organized, and focused on what you can do for them. The longest proposals rarely win. The ones that do are usually creative and memorable.

10

QUIT
OFFERING DISCOUNTS
EARLY IN THE GAME.

———

Don't give away the store. Seems like a no-brainer, right? You'd be surprised at how often it happens. Salespeople fall into the early discounting trap before potential customers even express concern about price. That's a Sales strategy that never works.

We get it: Pricing conversations are hard. For some salespeople, there's an uneasy feeling that comes over them in the split second before they quote a price. It's an emotional hesitation rooted in doubt. What if the price is too high? What if our competitors are making a better offer? What if this deal vanishes into thin air as soon as I toss out a number?

If those questions have made you flinch before, they can haunt you. Maybe you got nervous and immediately dropped the price. The customer jumped at the phenomenal offer. And then there was no one to blame for the shrinking commission but YOU.

Lowering your price before you get started is a strategy that will do nothing but cost you money and sales. Not to mention your reputation. It makes your pricing structure look phony and manipulative. In the speaking world, we could lose a lot of business if a customer discovered she paid full price for our services and the company across town got the same thing for 40% off. People talk. Don't risk it.

Here are three powerful reasons you should never throw out discounts until you've tried every other serious negotiation strategy:

a. **You lose your focus.** Pricing should be one of the last things discussed with a potential buyer. Concentrate first on understanding the needs you can meet with your product or service. Position yourself as the best solution. If you have created enough value and demonstrated potential ROI, then price won't be a deal-breaker.

b. **You set a bad precedent.** If your customer is price-sensitive and you offer an immediate discount, you have nowhere to go but down. Never box yourself into a corner that ensures low profit long-term.

c. **You give away the incentive for loyalty.** Discounts should be earned, not automatically included. Save something to reward your customers for sticking with you over time.

d. **You devalue your product and service.** If you doubt the worth of your product, so will your customers. Fee integrity is essential.

SALES TAKEAWAY

Help customers see that what you offer is worth every penny. Protect your margin, and don't let your doubts force you into discounting when you don't need to or have to.

⓫
QUIT
AVOIDING THE UPSELL OR CROSS-SELL.

———

Sometimes salespeople assume they know everything about their customers' needs and wants. (No finger-pointing there; we used to do it, too!) Unfortunately, that assumption could cost them money. A ton of it. Why? Because they aren't making the effort to upsell or cross-sell.

In our experiences, customers can get in a rut buying certain things from the same supplier, and they don't even know what else that supplier offers. At the same time, salespeople get in a groove of promoting their top-selling products, so they skip right over the other options. And, if we're keeping it real here, sometimes the salespeople just don't want to rock the boat by asking for more.

Does that hesitancy resonate with you? In your efforts to build relationships with customers, you may not want to appear greedy. A hard push to keep adding on to the bill might undermine trust. And once you lose trust, the game is over. It somehow seems safer to get the signature on the dotted line — and get out before they have a change of heart.

Our recommendation? Slow down. Recognize that you've already completed the hardest part of the sale. You scored a meeting. Engaged them in conversation. Persuaded them of the benefits. And actually got them to buy. Don't let that go to waste! With all that hard work behind you, why walk away from the additional sales that could come from upselling and cross-selling?

Let's start with upselling, for instance. When customers are buying from you, take time to think about the additional products or services that would naturally go along with the purchase. If it makes business sense for the customer, describe how the bigger "bundle" could produce better results or a stronger return on investment.

As for cross-selling, think outside the box. Use whatever insights you gained about the customer in closing the initial deal to discover fresh ways to meet their needs. That solution could come in the form of a completely different product line or even a strategic partnership with another department. Get creative!

When you invest the time to help your customers come up with innovative ways to solve their problems, you'll create new opportunities for them to do business with you. And best of all, you'll build loyal relationships that translate into greater sales.

SALES TAKEAWAY

Don't hesitate to offer your customers the "extras" that will add value to your initial sale. Upselling and cross-selling are lucrative, so adopt the perspective that you're helping your customers solve additional problems. Not padding the bill.

12

QUIT
FAILING TO RECOGNIZE
THE POWER OF SILENCE.

The gift of gab is fairly common among salespeople. When they get a foot in the door to meet with potential customers, they want to use every single moment to talk. To sell. To promote their products. To make a connection. To share stories. And while being talkative can be a strength for any salesperson, *silence* is actually a negotiation strategy that is far more valuable (and remarkably underused).

All things considered, we know that silence can sometimes feel uncomfortable. Maybe even painful for some people. For those who prefer wall-to-wall dialogue in every conversation, there's an underlying compulsion to jump in and fill the wasted verbal space with helpful facts or insightful statements. Anything to prevent an awkward lull.

In reality, a bit of silence is a positive thing. Just to be clear, we're not talking about long, gaping holes in the conversation, but momentary breaks that give the interaction a little breathing room. Creating silence offers space for your prospects to speak. The more they talk, the more you listen, and the more you'll learn about exactly what they need, what they want, and what it will take to get them to buy.

Here are four reasons why silence can give you a distinct Sales advantage:

a. **Silence signals that you are listening.** After you've quickly established control and set the tone, allow your prospects to do the talking. Make sure they feel heard, not rushed. You may uncover valuable information that helps you customize your product to better meet their needs. Honestly, they probably want to talk about themselves as much as you do.

b. **Silence gives prospects time to think.** They may need a moment to consider what you've said. To form an opinion. To think of some pertinent questions. Give them that mental space to process the facts and contemplate how this potential relationship could add value for their businesses.

c. **Silence shows respect.** Your Sales presentation should be a dialogue rather than a monologue. Pausing can be perceived as an invitation for the prospect to join the conversation and increase the interaction. It's a sign of courtesy that opens the door for two-way communication.

d. **Silence demonstrates strength.** Wait patiently for a response after stating your offer. If you interpret that silence as an objection (or a rejection), you may find yourself offering discounts and freebies that aren't necessary.

SALES TAKEAWAY

Get comfortable with silence. When you're constantly figuring out what to say at the very next pause, you aren't listening. Take a breath and relax.

13

QUIT
WAITING FOR BUYERS TO
GET BACK IN TOUCH WITH YOU.

We have all been there. We had a phenomenal meeting with a prospect who was definitely interested in moving forward. All the signs were positive. There was excitement about the product. Praise for our presentation. And an enthusiastic promise to get right back to us. We assume it's a done deal. All we have to do is sit back and wait for the official "thumbs up."

Then…total silence. Nothing but crickets. We hesitate to make the next move because they said they would get back to us when everything was ready. Our advice? Don't fall for that! Not for one minute. If you wait, chances are, you may never hear from them again. Fact is, you've totally given away control of the Sales process.

Here's one of the key Sales strategies we teach when working with clients: To close the sale, you have to take charge. And that means being crystal clear about defining the next Sales discussion.

Just like you, prospects get busy. The realities of business get in the way. Their best employee quits. They have a crisis with one of their own customers. The IT network crashes. No matter how extraordinary your Sales presentation was, calling you back suddenly falls to the very bottom of their to-do list.

To avoid any confusion, THIS is the message every salesperson needs to hear: Never, ever, ever assume they will get back to you. That's *your* job. With that said, following up with potential customers requires a certain level of finesse to avoid veering into the "annoying lane." These quick tips may help you accomplish that:

a. **Clarify the process.** Ask smart questions. How many people are involved in the final decision? Is there a committee? How much time do they need to review the options? What could potentially slow things down (budget uncertainty, people out of the office, etc.)? How can you accommodate those issues to help stay on track?

b. **Own the next step.** Maintain control of the process by clearly taking responsibility for what comes next. They'll be expecting your follow-up – and you won't be waiting for them to make a move.

c. **Tie it down.** Set a specific date for your next discussion, and get it scheduled. Promptly send out a calendar invite. Confirm as it gets closer.

d. **Be gracious.** If the prospect is clearly not interested, let it go. Continuing to push is rude and annoying.

SALES TAKEAWAY

Always control the sale by making sure the next move with a legitimate potential client is YOURS. That's an essential component, whether the customer relationship is brand new or long term.

14

QUIT

HESITATING TO ASK FOR THE BUSINESS.

You do all the tedious, lead-generation work. Make numerous phone calls. Leave messages. Call back. Find the right prospect. Set up the appointments. Build trust. And sell your heart out. Whew! You'd think the final step in the Sales process – *asking for the business* – would be obvious, right? Sadly, you'd be wrong.

Time and time again, we find good salespeople who assume that all the preliminary steps were "enough." Which leads us to ask: WHY? Why would someone go to that much trouble and then allow the sale to disappear or, worse yet, go to the competition?

The only way to get the business is ASK FOR IT! That's the most important step in the whole process. Without that closure, there will often be NO SALE.

Never assume that your customers know you *want* their business. Never assume that they will make the first move. Never assume that you'll offend them by being direct. And never assume that subtle hints will be enough to make them take the bait. You can't run the football the entire length of the field and drop it on the one-yard line. It's close. But it doesn't count. Don't drop the ball on a sale that's 99% finished!

So exactly why do Sales professionals hesitate to ask for the business? Here are the most common reasons we see:

a. They lack confidence in themselves.

b. They don't believe in their products.

c. They never bothered to truly connect with the customer and build trust.

d. They don't want to look too pushy or make anyone angry.

e. They believe that leading a horse to water is enough to make him drink (even though we know how that saying goes).

f. They gave the customer control of the conversation and next steps.

g. They are flat-out afraid to ask in case the answer is NO.

Reality check: Hearing "no" is part of Sales. It's a fact. A given. Happens all the time. Being afraid of hearing "no" is probably preventing you from hearing "yes." Accept that asking for the business is part of your job as a Sales professional. Then just do it!

SALES TAKEAWAY

Develop the kind of relationships with your prospects that make asking for the business easy. Natural. Even obvious. But don't skip the last step: Ask for the order! If you don't, your competitors will.

15

QUIT

USING CHEESY CLOSING STRATEGIES.

————

Imagine being served an elegant, delicious meal prepared by a talented chef. But when it's time for dessert, you receive a half-eaten box of stale cookies. It doesn't match up. All of the time and effort invested in the first part of the experience was ruined by a bad choice at the very end. That's essentially what happens when good salespeople get sidetracked with closing gimmicks.

The pitch starts out with great promise. Salespeople might be diligent about doing research and carefully preparing for the meeting. They deliver a compelling presentation that succinctly explains how their products are the perfect solutions for the potential buyers' problems. Everything seems to be right on track until the salesperson trots out a cheesy, overused closing strategy that tanks the whole thing. We'd love to say this fatal misstep is rare, but that's not the case.

Ever heard these? Or (cringe!) ever used one of them?

a. **Free Give-Away:** Buy today, and you'll get a free bonus!
b. **30-Day Trial:** Say yes today, and you can try the product for a month with no cost or obligation!

c. **Limited-Time Offer:** Buy today, because this deal won't be around much longer!

d. **Price-Hike Alert:** Sign up today to lock in your price before it goes up!

e. **Money-Back Guarantee:** Buy today with no risk!

Besides transforming a professional presentation into something from the Home Shopping Network, these closing gimmicks erode credibility. They sound manipulative. And, most importantly, they could undermine everything you've said up to that point.

If you've done your job to demonstrate the value your product can provide, customers won't be swayed by a free offer. It's not necessary. And if you and your organization are known for integrity, it's a "given" that you will stand behind your products. If there's a problem, you'll make it right. Customers expect that, so it's almost surprising to tout a money-back guarantee. Why would someone do business with you if they felt like they were buying a clearance item at the post-holiday sale with no returns and no exchanges? Stick to selling value, and skip the gimmicks.

SALES TAKEAWAY

Prove that your products are the perfect fit. Build relationships. But don't degrade your offer by throwing in gimmicks at the last minute. Your carefully prepared presentation could start to sound like a late-night infomercial. And that could cost you the sale.

16

QUIT
REFUSING TO WALK AWAY.

If salespeople give up easily, they won't be in Sales for very long. Perseverance often wins the race in this industry. So making the decision to walk away from a prospect with nothing to show for your efforts can be painful. It hurts the ego as much as the wallet.

And yet, sometimes that's the smartest choice. The most successful salespeople understand that wasting time on a deal that's an endless struggle means they aren't focusing on the leads and customers that are much more likely to result in a signed contract. They balance perseverance with the ability to know when to cut their losses.

Here are some helpful guidelines for determining when it's best to just say "no":

a. **Work to improve your close ratio.** When we coach Sales teams, one of the first things we do is help them increase their close ratio — the number of successful sales compared with the number of leads contacted over a certain period of time. The bottom line is, you can't and won't close the deal with every single prospect. Be willing to admit when you don't have the right solution. If it becomes perfectly clear that your products are not a good fit for a customer, move on to find another one that is.

b. **Recognize the red flags.** If the process of trying to close the deal is like pulling teeth, you can bet this high-maintenance relationship is going to drive you crazy long term. You can spend your time on a painfully difficult customer or reserve your energy (and patience) for relationships that are happier and much more profitable. Your stress level will be better by choosing the latter.

c. **Know when to disqualify a prospect.** Watch for the signs that your contact person doesn't really have the authority, incentive, or money to make the purchase. Does this person seem unaware of the exact project needs, the deadline, or who else will be involved in making the decision? If you continue hearing, *"I don't know,"* then it's time to find someone else who does.

d. **Don't become a creepy stalker.** If the prospect doesn't return your calls after you've reached out a few times, STOP! Take the hint. By graciously respecting those boundaries, you can leave the door open for sales in the future, should the situation change. That's an unlikely outcome if you've ventured into restraining-order territory with your aggressive follow-up.

SALES TAKEAWAY

Estimate your chances of closing each deal, and rank your prospects accordingly. Use that as a guide for organizing your days. If a potential buyer starts taking up a disproportionate amount of time, weigh the options of moving on.

17

QUIT

BELIEVING THE CLOSE IS THE END.

———————

Just as this book is definitely NOT the end of your journey toward greater success in Sales, closing the deal with the big client doesn't mean your Sales job is complete. In reality, it's just the beginning. How's that for a different perspective? It can be tempting to think about the signature on the contract as the pinnacle of Sales success, but that's really just the ceremonial wave of the checkered flag at the starting line.

Now it's time to show what you're really made of. We're talking about follow-up here. Serious, focused, committed, ongoing customer care. The kind that transforms a single sale into a loyal, lifelong customer – YOUR customer.

Not to heap on the pressure here, but this is a fact worth noting: The fate of all future sales with this particular customer's organization depends on the relationship you develop and nurture. In building your reputation as a valuable partner, you also become the "face" of your company for that customer. Strengthen that bond, and additional business will come your way.

Here are three of our favorite tips for ensuring that you create long-term customers.

a. **Ask them how you can continue to add value.** We recommend having conversations with your customers to discover how you can best serve them moving forward. Would it be helpful for you to provide additional product details? Timely news about the industry? Information about other services you offer that could help them reach their goals? You have an opportunity to position yourself as a valuable resource instead of simply a product provider.

b. **Personalize your approach.** Salespeople often have a standard follow-up strategy that works most of the time, and they apply it to everyone. Not a smart move since every customer is different. Make sure you know the customers' budget cycles and ordering patterns so you can schedule timely contacts.

c. **Determine their preferred method of communication.** What's the best way for you to contact them? And how often? Ask them directly. We have customers who love email – and ones who never check email but respond to a text message in a nanosecond. Others would much rather receive a good, old-fashioned phone call. Forego the communication style that's easiest for you, and cater to the customers' preferences.

SALES TAKEAWAY

Closing the sale is really the beginning of a whole new relationship. Work to strengthen those connections instead of getting distracted by the next opportunity on the horizon.

CONCLUSION

There you have it: Sales wisdom from every angle. Sixty chapters. Hundreds of strategies. One crystal-clear purpose – to help you increase sales, attract new customers, strengthen your professional relationships, expand your market share, and make more money. *Significantly more.*

And all of that comes from the choice to quit doing the things that are undermining your success.

You may have intuitively known about some of these behaviors and attitudes that could be holding you back. Or you have learned about them the hard way, by losing customers and losing money. But, if you're like most salespeople, you've also uncovered some hidden roadblocks in these pages. Things you never thought about before. Things you need to quit. Today. Right now.

If you want to be the kind of salesperson who customers would fight to buy from, don't let these realizations go to waste. Commit to the change.

It's time to let go of:

The beliefs that are destroying your Sales potential.
The excuses that are getting in your way with customers.
The assumptions that are costing you big money.
The traits that are preventing you from closing more deals.
The negotiation tactics that are diminishing your power.

And once you make the decision to STOP doing those things? You'll START moving your Sales career forward at an accelerated pace. Bigger clients. Larger contracts. Enhanced business relationships. Improved customer loyalty. And, the ultimate benefit, more financial success and the rewards that come with it.

We feel confident that you'll experience the bottom-line value of applying the strategies we've shared. When you cut through the obstacles and embrace these new behaviors, be prepared to send your sales right through the roof.

How cool is that?!?

Wait! One more thing… Before you determine it's not necessary to read the flip side of this book because you aren't in management, we want to change your mind! If you apply the strategies you just learned, your extraordinary Sales success will likely position you as a prime candidate for a leadership position in the future. And besides, how many times have you wondered what in the world your Sales leader does all day? Read the other section to find out. You might be surprised at the answer!

ABOUT
Connie Podesta

Connie is a Hall of Fame international keynote speaker, an award-winning author of nine books, and an expert in the Psychology of Sales and Human Behavior. Connie is known for being a game-changing, sales-generating, leadership-developing, revenue-building ball of fire. Her rare blend of laugh-out-loud humor, amazing insights, convention-defying substance and no-nonsense style have made her a consistently in-demand business and Sales speaker for more than 25 years.

Voted **One of the Top Motivational Speakers to Energize Sales Teams** by *Resourceful Selling* magazine, Connie is famous for dazzling her audiences with unforgettable, reality-based strategies that inspire them to take bold action. She also empowers these salespeople to dynamically change the way they approach every interaction, successfully taking on a new generation of customers who have more choices than ever before.

Other Books

Leadership…Like You've Never Heard It Before
10 Ways to Stand Out from the Crowd
Life Would Be Easy if it Weren't for Other People
Happiness is Serious Business
Selling to Women/Selling to Men
How to be the Person Successful Companies Would Fight to Keep
Audiences Stand Up When You Stand Out
Texting Harry

Connect

Email: **connie@conniepodesta.com**
Website: **www.ConniePodesta.com**
Phone: **(972) 596-5501**

f Connie Podesta Presents
in Connie Podesta
🐦 @Connie_Podesta
▶ Connie Podesta Presents

ABOUT
Meridith Elliott Powell

Named one of the *Top 15 Business Growth Experts To Watch* by *CurrencyFair,* Meridith is a highly acclaimed business growth expert, keynote speaker, and award-winning author. She coaches leaders to learn the Sales and growth strategies needed to help their organizations succeed, no matter what happens with the economy.

Known for her innovative content, wicked wit and high-energy style, Meridith was recently voted **One of the Top Motivational Speakers to Energize Sales Teams** by *Resourceful Selling* magazine. Meridith delivers compelling keynotes that have salespeople on the edge of their seats, fully engaged and ready to produce powerful results.

Other Books

Own It: Redefining Responsibility
Winning in the Trust and Value Economy
42 Rules to Turn Prospects into Customers
Mastering the Art of Success
The Confidence Plan

Online Courses

Own It: Redefining Responsibility
Sales: Selling Financial Products and Services
Consulting Foundations: Building Your Sales System
Selling into Industries: Manufacturing
Selling into Industries: Telecommunications
Soft Skills for Sales Professionals

Connect

Email: **mere@valuespeaker.com**
Website: **www.ValueSpeaker.com**
Phone: **(888) 526-9998**

Meridith Elliott Powell, CSP

Meridith Elliott Powell

@MeridithElliottPowell

Meridith Elliott Powell

THE BEST SALES LEADERSHIP BOOK EVER

CUT

Through the **OBSTACLES** *and*
CREATE A KILLER SALES TEAM

MERIDITH ELLIOTT POWELL
AND CONNIE PODESTA

STANDOUT Press
Dallas, Texas

DEDICATION

To the thousands of Sales leaders out there who work hard every day to enable team success. We know the challenges are intense. You're expected to train, coach, and mentor. Collaborate and inspire. Hold people accountable. Model the behaviors and attitudes required to be winning salespeople. And, of course, you take the heat if they fall short of their ambitious goals. The demands are overwhelming, but we've got you covered!

This book is dedicated to helping you take a deeper dive into the mindsets of your salespeople. Their personalities. Their perspectives. Their Sales styles. And once you're armed with those insights, you'll know exactly how to empower your team members to smash every Sales goal in their path. We know you can do it. We're ready to help!

TABLE OF CONTENTS

SECTION ONE:
Leadership Habits
that Sabotage a Winning Team

——————

SECTION TWO:
Leadership Behaviors
that Send the Wrong Message

——————

INTRODUCTION

Co-Author Q&A
With Meridith Elliott Powell (MEP) and Connie Podesta (CP)

This personal, behind-the-scenes conversation with the authors will give you some fascinating insights into the genesis of this book and its distinct purpose.

Meridith Elliott Powell
- *Business Growth Expert*
- *Acclaimed Keynote Speaker*
- *Award-Winning Author of 6 Books*
- *Master-Certified Business Strategist*
- *Executive Coach*
- *Online Course Instructor*
- *Former Sales Leader*

Connie Podesta
- *Sales & Leadership Psychology Expert*
- *Hall of Fame Keynote Speaker*
- *Award-Winning Author of 9 Books*
- *Elite Sales Strategist*
- *Comedienne*
- *Executive Coach*
- *Therapist*

Q: Why did Sales leadership warrant its own section of the book?

CP: We couldn't possibly write a comprehensive book about Sales without addressing the unique issues of Sales leadership. That's an integral part of the equation. If companies want to create high-impact Sales teams, they have to start by looking at the quality of their Sales leadership.

MEP: There's absolutely a direct link. The team is only as good as its leaders. In fact, when organizations invest more in their Sales leaders, their salespeople produce better results. Their win ratios are higher. Revenue goes up. They have a more consistent track record for surpassing Sales goals. Plus, the retention rate for top Sales talent is greatly improved. Sales leadership is the key to all of it.

CP: With all of that said, we also want to encourage every Sales leader to read the other section of this book designed for salespeople. The whole thing, beginning to end. Preferably first. That's critical information for them to know as they coach and mentor their teams, as well as for modeling success behaviors and traits that can lead to greater sales. If they want to hold their teams accountable for all of those foundational Sales skills, they need to understand them on the deepest possible level.

MEP: Sales leaders today are feeling increasingly overwhelmed by the demands and expectations of this job. Those have changed dramatically in recent years. With this book, we want to help Sales leaders focus their time and energy on the actions that will have the biggest impact on their teams' ability to achieve higher goals.

CP: In keeping with the other section of the book, we've approached this challenge by highlighting things that Sales leaders need to quit doing to become more successful. They need to figure out what's holding them back and be willing to let those things go. To support that, we provide a concise, candid discussion about the leadership habits and behaviors that are critical for those who lead teams of salespeople. It's very targeted. And it's designed to help them accelerate results in a dramatic way.

Q: What do each of you bring to the table in this area?

MEP: Connie has extensive experience in Sales and leadership, but she also has a background as a therapist and counselor. She's an expert in human behavior. That means she knows Sales from the inside out. She understands the psychology behind it. In this book, she shows leaders how to get inside the minds of their salespeople to improve development and inspire better performance. It's a fascinating perspective.

CP: As for Meridith, she is a former Sales executive who has also spent years successfully coaching other Sales leaders. She has firsthand knowledge of the challenges involved in this job and knows the Sales industry from every angle. The skills. The systems. The processes. She has brilliant insights on the strategies and tactics that Sales leaders can use to elevate the performance of their teams.

MEP: Sales leadership really is both an art and a science. By combining our different areas of expertise, we were able to cover this topic in a fresh way.

CP: It certainly is a unique approach. This has been a very strong partnership, and we think our readers will benefit from this collaboration.

LEADERSHIP HABITS...
THAT SABOTAGE A WINNING TEAM

Before your
salespeople are
willing to up their game,
you've got to sell them
on following your lead.

1
QUIT
ACTING LIKE A BOSS.

Do your salespeople follow your lead because they WANT to? Or because they HAVE to? If they *choose* to follow you because they respect, admire and believe in you, their chances of achieving increased productivity, sales, and market share will soar. If they are following you out of a sense of obligation, complacency or fear, their sales production is destined for a big drop. And that giant plunge will show up in YOUR numbers as their leader.

Let's explore the contrast. A boss demands respect, while a leader commands it. Psychologically, people who get bossed around without much buy-in or consensus usually push back. Maybe even do the exact opposite of what's being demanded. Not a good scenario as Sales goals escalate and Sales numbers plummet.

To succeed as the leader of a Sales team, you've got to make the commitment to act like (and be recognized as) a leader — and quit acting like a boss. But first, make sure you understand the nuances involved:

a. **Leaders are people-focused. Bosses are task-focused.**
   The biggest asset of any Sales team is its people — the ones

out there making the sales. Leaders stay focused on the people, while bosses get hopelessly sidetracked by paperwork, policies, and projections.

b. **Leaders support and energize. Bosses order and demand.** To keep salespeople fueled for the tough job ahead, leaders supply assistance and encouragement. Bosses bark out orders and threats that create resistance and resentment.

c. **Leaders focus on what went right. Bosses focus on what went wrong.** Mistakes are going to happen. Deals will fall through. But when a salesperson faces adversity, the manager's response can change everything. Instead of blaming like a boss, a great leader looks for ways to fix the problem and create learning opportunities for the future.

d. **Leaders share the credit. Bosses take the credit.** Bosses love to hog the spotlight, even though Sales teams generally do the heavy lifting out in the field. Leaders intuitively understand that highlighting others' achievements will contribute to greater team success and a more impressive ROI.

e. **Leaders show people what to do. Bosses tell them.** Salespeople want to be led by someone who has mastered the industry, knows the game, and has played it exceptionally well. They want a relatable role model.

SALES LEADERSHIP TAKEAWAY

Adopt the mindset of a leader rather than a boss as you manage and inspire your Sales team. You'll strengthen your bottom-line results *and* your employees will WANT to follow your lead. That makes all the difference in the world.

② QUIT

ACCEPTING THE STATUS QUO.

———————

Sometimes the greatest innovations aren't *revolutionary*; they're *evolutionary*. They involve new ways of making older products better, faster, easier, smarter, more efficient, less boring, or more affordable. Whew! If you can help your Sales team to embrace that concept, you may establish a new path for gaining a competitive advantage.

Rather than always waiting for R&D to go through the long process of creating new products, what if you inspired your Sales team to take the lead once in a while? It's possible! You can teach your team to look at the intersection between your customers' challenges and your products in a more innovative way.

As these salespeople communicate with existing and potential customers, they are in the prime position to spot hidden opportunities for product innovation. They hear firsthand what buyers want. What they don't want. What works and what doesn't. Which products they really need that don't yet exist. If Sales professionals are paying attention, they may discover clues for innovation with every phone call, email, or face-to-face meeting.

There's a massive gold mine of ideas in those conversations! But those ideas are only valuable if salespeople listen and bring them back to the folks in Marketing or Development. To help your Sales professionals become status-quo crushers, follow these guidelines:

a. **Emphasize product knowledge.** Make sure your team members know the specific strengths and weaknesses of your product. Prompt them to think harder about how the product matches customer needs. What could be changed or tweaked for a closer fit?

b. **Focus on customer experience.** Encourage your salespeople to ask customers more probing questions about the process of buying and using your products. What's missing? What's irrelevant? What could be better?

c. **Think about solutions.** Remind them to be problem solvers, not product sellers. When they learn to think big picture, they're more likely to uncover tiny seeds of innovation.

d. **Make innovation a priority.** Provide incentives for salespeople to bring back ideas based on customer feedback. Build excitement about participating in the process, and reward those who step up to help define a new competitive advantage.

SALES LEADERSHIP TAKEAWAY

Help your salespeople buck the status quo by using the customer experience to spark innovation. By asking strategic questions, they can identify hidden opportunities that increase the value they bring to their customers and to your organization.

3

QUIT

HIRING THE WRONG PEOPLE.

Having the greatest products on the planet doesn't guarantee success. But having the best team of people to sell those products can come pretty close. If you lead a Sales department, one of your most important tasks is hiring the right individuals to be the external face of your company – interacting with your customers and attracting new ones. In other words, your ability to assess, recognize, and recruit high-potential Sales talent will determine the success or failure of your team. Kind of intimidating when you think about it that way, huh? It's a fact.

Ask any Sales managers who have rushed to hire someone – anyone! – to cover an open territory. Those "shortcuts" often saddled them with lackluster sales, bad attitudes, prickly co-worker relationships, and customer complaints. How about the stress of letting them go and the time involved to hire and train someone new? Not a good trade-off. At all. The quick relief of having that territory covered was replaced with hassles and headaches that lasted for months after those marginal employees moved on.

How can you make sure you're hiring the RIGHT salespeople? First, upgrade your attitude. Don't start the hiring process with negative or self-destructive thinking: *"It's a tough time to hire right now.*

All of our competitors are looking for new salespeople, too. We're going to have to take whatever we can get."

When leaders hire from a place of desperation, they spend their interviews begging people to take the job – and end up with a staff of underwhelming underperformers. Remind yourself of the value you have to offer. Create an atmosphere of success that gets applicants excited to be part of your Sales team. Make THEM sell YOU. Not the other way around.

Second, upgrade your expectations. When you create a list of preferred qualifications, be clear and aim higher than describing an "average" salesperson. Raise the bar! If you have to give up on a few ideal characteristics, you can still choose a new hire who's a fast learner. Elevate the quality of your search, and you'll dramatically expand the quality of your Sales team.

Third, prepare to hire before you need to. Just like the best potential customers are already doing business with someone else, the best salespeople already have a job. Scope them out. Be proactive about starting to court them. And be patient: Hiring the best may take some time.

SALES LEADERSHIP TAKEAWAY

Hire from a place of confidence and success – before you are desperate for new talent. Raise your standards, and stick to them. It may take some time to win over the right people, but the ROI is well worth the effort.

4

QUIT
LOWERING YOUR STANDARDS.

Assembling a kick-butt Sales team is NOT an easy task. We've worked with hundreds of Sales leaders and, far too often, we discover that their teams end up with two types of salespeople:

"He is such a great guy, and the customers love him. Just wish he could get his numbers up and meet his goals."

"She is incredible. No one closes a deal like she does. But, for some reason, customers often request a different Sales representative after she wraps things up."

It's a classic battle: Hiring those who have loads of personality and charisma versus those who know how to negotiate, ask for the money, and close the deal. If you want to build a team that exceeds goals every time, you need to find salespeople who have the ability to connect with customers AND the talent to get results. If you settle for one or the other, you're reducing your team's potential before you ever get started. Sales leaders don't usually set out to lower their standards in that way; it just happens.

Short of hiring all-new Sales hotshots who can build relationships and sell up a storm, your task as the Sales leader is to nurture both types of characteristics among your existing salespeople.

The easiest place to start is by exhibiting your respect and passion for Sales at every turn. Your team is a reflection of YOU. Through coaching, training and mentoring, you can SHOW them how to build a better Sales pipeline, create a seamless follow-up system, and polish off their negotiating skills.

Trying to help salespeople make improvements to their personalities, attitudes, and confidence levels is a much bigger mountain to climb. Many of those attributes are inherent, representing thought processes and behaviors they've used since childhood. Those conversations can be tough, but they can also be a gift if they are handled with compassion and encouragement. Be fair, and speak up. The payoff will be making better personality matches between your customers and salespeople for higher-quality relationships.

As the leader, just remember that your best route to Sales success is finding salespeople who bring the whole package to the table. Don't lower your standards and settle for just anyone. Be intentional about finding the right people with the right qualifications for your team. Work to help your existing employees become more balanced. That's the key to creating a dynamic, versatile team of top performers.

SALES LEADERSHIP TAKEAWAY

Recognize that your salespeople need to have the ability to connect AND the ability to sell. One or the other isn't enough. Don't settle for less.

5

QUIT

FAILING TO USE TARGETED INTERVIEW STRATEGIES.

———————

Companies often expect Sales leaders to participate in professional development. To improve presentation skills. Master the latest coaching techniques. Expand strategic thinking. But there's one area that is frequently missing from the list of required learning. Most Sales leaders aren't given much (if any) interview training. Which leaves us flabbergasted, since the human resources component of Sales is the most critical. That's where everything starts. Or ends.

Here are our best tips for creating a successful, sustainable, full-funnel interview strategy that will engage and attract the highest-performing salespeople – and help you weed out the worst.

a. **Use short, open-ended questions.** If you toss the ball into their court without a lot of prompting, you'll be able to see their intuitive abilities and how they verbally explore to find out what you're really looking for. That's exactly the kind of conversational techniques they'll need with customers.

b. **Repeat the process.** Using the same questions with each applicant will allow you to compare answers, attitudes, and reactions. All candidates have unique backgrounds, so additional questions may be required to fully understand their backstories. But if you keep the core questions the same, you'll have a more objective way to analyze the interview results when it's time to make a choice.

c. **Incorporate role play.** Potential applicants can vividly describe how they'd handle a certain Sales situation, but that's not the same thing as seeing them in action. Pretend to be the customer, and ask them to sell you one of your products. (Great way to determine whether they have done their homework!) Pay close attention to their behaviors, body language, and tones of voice. Throw out plenty of excuses NOT to buy, and see how they respond in tough situations.

d. **Ask for examples.** Get them talking about their experience and stories of serving previous customers. What challenges did they face? How did they solve them?

e. **Be observant.** How do the applicants dress, speak, behave, and carry themselves? Were they late? Are they argumentative? Evasive? Less than engaging? Presumably, they will never be better than they are in the job interview.

f. **Watch how they sell themselves.** Are they persuasive in convincing you to hire them? Notice their communication styles and the way they build a case for getting the job. How do they handle questions or objections? Do they try to close the deal? Most importantly, are you buying it?

SALES LEADERSHIP TAKEAWAY

Prequalify your applicants just like you prequalify your Sales leads. Use strategic interview techniques to help you identify the best hires with the greatest potential to increase the performance of your Sales team.

6

QUIT

LEADING EVERYONE THE SAME WAY.

As if leading a Sales team couldn't be any more complex and multifaceted, the task is made increasingly daunting by the fact that every salesperson brings a unique personality to the mix. Some leaders don't take the time to consider the impact, and they fall for what we describe as the Golden Rule Trap. We'll explain.

As children, most of us were taught "the golden rule": We should treat others the way we want to be treated. Definitely a great mantra for life. The world needs more kindness and consideration. No arguments there. But as *Sales leaders,* this deeply ingrained belief could be inadvertently reducing our effectiveness.

If we treat all our team members the way *we* want to be treated, we are automatically assuming their preferences and needs are exactly the same as ours. That assumption could be driving everything about the way we approach the leadership role. How we communicate. Collaborate. Motivate. Mentor. Provide feedback. The whole enchilada.

But we're following the golden rule, so it must be a great strategy. Right? In this case, no. We could be operating from the faulty belief that *our* way is the *best* way – and everyone else will

13

The Best Sales Leadership Book Ever

surely love and appreciate our personal style as a leader. Which may or may not be true. It's a hidden trap disguised as being thoughtful and considerate.

So what's the solution? To improve your effectiveness, adjust your leadership style for your team members in the same way you might adjust to a customer's buying style during a sale. Get to know them. Are they right-brained (more creative and artistic)? Left-brained (more analytical and methodical)? Or somewhere in the middle? Are they extroverts (outgoing and social)? Introverts (work well on their own)? Or ambiverts (a mix of both)?

As a leader, it's your job to figure out what you can do to help your salespeople reach their full potential. One team member might prefer a just-the-facts, cut-to-the-chase approach to conversations, while another wants to know that you care about his weekend plans and latest hobby. Consider *what they need,* rather than *what you would want.* Through your willingness to adapt your style to their needs, you can gain a significant advantage in the quest to improve their engagement, commitment, and Sales performance.

Treating others the way you want to be treated is a great rule for life. But as a Sales leader, you can reach higher levels of success if you quit leading all of your salespeople the same way.

SALES LEADERSHIP TAKEAWAY

Work to understand the different personalities on your team, and use that to fine-tune your leadership style and communication. The added effort will pay off.

14

7

QUIT
MICROMANAGING YOUR TEAM.

We've coached plenty of salespeople over the years who weren't happy with their jobs. The number one complaint? Micromanaging! It's not just annoying. It's also one of the main reasons why salespeople quit. By their very nature, salespeople have an independent streak. OK, *some* of them may have authority issues. But *all* of them really, really hate feeling scrutinized at every turn. It's demoralizing. If you want to get the most out of your Sales team, hire the right people and give them the space to do their jobs.

From a business standpoint, micromanaging could be a complete disaster — for you, your salespeople, your company, and your customers. Here's why:

a. **It demonstrates a lack of trust.** When salespeople sense that you feel the need to observe and control every move they make, they don't feel trusted. That can lead to resentment and anger. Besides, micromanaging undermines their confidence and decreases their incentive to produce and succeed.

b. **It puts the spotlight on problems.** Leaders who incessantly micromanage are never satisfied. They are always looking for faults and missed opportunities, highlighting the negative rather than the positive. That's a productivity killer.

c. **It creates a tense environment.** Micromanagers may take pride in finding things that need correcting – as though it's evidence of how smart they are. Unfortunately, that makes salespeople feel defensive and leads them to hide their mistakes rather than risk being reprimanded.

d. **It takes too much time.** When leaders demand to know complete details about every action taken and decision made by their salespeople, they get bogged down in the minutiae. Projects drag out, and teams lose momentum.

e. **It dilutes leadership.** Micromanagers get in the way of their own success. When their time and attention are diverted by tasks way below their pay grade, they fail to notice what's happening on a higher level. Don't abdicate your leadership role. And if you're managing people who require constant babysitting, it's time to set boundaries. Hold them accountable, and let the consequences fall as deserved.

f. **It's unproductive.** Stop telling yourself that micromanaging is just a necessary evil to make your team more productive. That's not true. It's unproductive for you AND your team members. It's also the fastest way to set your team back and weaken your results.

SALES LEADERSHIP TAKEAWAY

Show your salespeople that you believe in them by letting them have an appropriate amount of independence. If you *don't*, you're displaying a lack of trust that will seriously block their chances of success. And if you *can't*, it's time to rethink your hiring choices.

8

QUIT

USING MANIPULATION
TO ACHIEVE HIGH RESULTS.

Communicating with your Sales team involves many different facets. Informing. Educating. Motivating. But all leaders get to choose how they want to approach those communication tasks. Sadly, some of them don't always make great choices.

Have you ever known Sales managers who communicated by yelling, threatening, criticizing, using sarcasm, or evoking guilt? Maybe even giving people the silent treatment? Those manipulative techniques are often accompanied by hidden agendas, endless game-playing, and a total lack of transparency. Not exactly contenders for the Leader of the Year award.

Oddly enough, these childish ploys may *initially* prompt team members to work harder. They are willing to do anything to avoid the embarrassment of being singled out by their leaders for non-performance. But in the long run? Trust us, those salespeople are desperately searching for the exit doors like people trapped in a burning building. They want out. IMMEDIATELY.

Feeling abused and mistreated does NOT create a foundation for hard work, positive attitudes, or increased sales. It does, however, raise the odds that those salespeople will spend the bulk of their workdays refreshing their resumes and searching for a more positive employment situation.

If there's any possible chance that manipulation has crept in to your team communications, make the choice to snuff that out. It doesn't work. Instead it works against you. Reboot your approach.

The goal is to create an open, healthy environment where your team members can prospect, meet with clients, create solutions, and close productive deals. And you can support them by sharing insightful ideas about the products, the organization, and even new Sales techniques to help them become more successful.

Salespeople want leaders who are role models – people who demonstrate how to be strong, productive, trustworthy, collaborative, and innovative professionals. Being manipulative negates all of that. If you really want your team to produce outstanding results, don't use a shortsighted approach.

SALES LEADERSHIP TAKEAWAY

Understand that the influence you have over your team and the results you produce as a leader are directly linked to the way you act and the strategies you use to communicate. YOUR behaviors drive THEIR level of engagement and performance.

9
QUIT
ACCEPTING EXCUSES.

_____

When your salespeople come to you with excuses disguised as legitimate reasons why they can't close deals, consider where they are placing the blame. Heard any of these? Our prices are too high. The competitor's products are better. The economy is awful. Our brand doesn't have enough recognition. Marketing gives us terrible leads. The Service Department keeps messing up.

The list of excuses used by salespeople can be distressingly long. And many items on the list can be painted to seem very plausible. But we're here to tell you: Don't fall for that!

If you've established yourself as a leader who accepts those excuses, you've already sent the signal that mediocrity is perfectly fine. At some point, you need to identify the real reason why sales aren't closing. And many times, it's the SALESPEOPLE. Truth? The buyers didn't like them or trust them enough to form a relationship and make the purchase. Tough to admit.

When Sales leaders refuse to hold their salespeople accountable, chaos emerges. Goals aren't met. Communications break down. Morale drops. Customers are lost. Trust disappears. In other words, accountability is everything! Shutting down the excuses should be a top priority.

Sales leaders who find success at the highest levels are committed to holding themselves and their teams accountable for the results they deliver. They realize that negativity and shifting the blame just erodes the energy and optimism needed to prospect, connect, negotiate, and close deals. To fight that erosion, they check to make sure each salesperson is attitudinally on the right track and help them turn excuses into action statements:

"I didn't ask the right questions, but I know what to do next time."
"I was too aggressive, and they backed off. I need to read my customers better."
"I got hung up on price. I need to focus on selling the value."
"I had a gut feeling the client wasn't going to buy, and I still spent way too much time there. I have to qualify my leads better."

When you make accountability a standard business practice for your salespeople, you'll begin to see them owning up to their missteps and moving forward with new strategies to close future deals. Your team members will grow. And your team's production will astound you.

SALES LEADERSHIP TAKEAWAY

Refuse to accept excuses from your salespeople, and demonstrate the power of accountability. When your team members feel personally responsible for their wins and losses, they will step up to achieve remarkable results.

10

QUIT

FAILING TO CONFRONT
PERFORMANCE ISSUES.

Many people think of confrontation as a zero-sum game. For one person to win, the other has to lose. Two potential outcomes. And no one wants to be a loser. Psychologically speaking, there are actually three possible ways that Sales leaders can respond to any situation with their direct reports: with positive feedback, with negative feedback, or with avoidance.

You can bet that Sales managers are "all in" for heaping on praise and positive reinforcement when their salespeople hit a home run. On the flip side, they may feel obligated to speak up and correct any salespeople who make serious mistakes. But, let's face it, there's an enormous gray area in between those options. Confronting salespeople about every minor infraction or rule-bending episode may seem downright uncomfortable – and what if it distracts them from selling at full force?

For the sake of the numbers, many Sales leaders prefer to overlook almost anything rather than confront the high producers. *"He drives the support staff crazy, and he never attends team events. But he brings in big clients. Why should I risk ruffling his feathers?"*

Time for the truth. Avoiding a problem is the same thing as consenting, giving in, or allowing the problem to continue. In other words, saying and doing nothing is often the loudest feedback of all. And now YOU – as the leader – are a partner in the ongoing problem. Even worse, you'll lose the respect of the others on your team who are working hard to do their jobs the right way.

Keep in mind: *confrontation* doesn't mean being disrespectful, rude, or mean-spirited. Sales leaders simply cannot be successful without a mindset that reframes confrontation as a normal part of business and a potential win/win opportunity. Ignoring difficult people and situations only compounds the problems, making them even harder to deal with down the road.

When we share our strategies with top Sales leaders, we remind them that they have a responsibility to be the problem solvers. They need to be willing and able to identify conflict brewing within their teams. To handle it professionally, even if that means having tough conversations. Some level of confrontation is necessary to keep a team operating at its peak level. Don't avoid it. And if you don't have the skills to do that gracefully, make it a priority to learn how.

SALES LEADERSHIP TAKEAWAY

Embrace the role of problem solver for your Sales team. Instead of avoiding confrontation, accept that some conflict is necessary. Face tough situations and people head on to help your team succeed.

11

QUIT
PENALIZING TOP PERFORMERS.

You're probably thinking that sounds preposterous. You do everything in your power to keep those high flyers happy, right? Stay with us here. What if you are penalizing them *unintentionally?* That's an issue you need to address.

Start by looking at the salespeople on the bottom end of the performance scale. That's where you'll find those who may suffer from bad attitudes and a lack of motivation. Theoretically, Sales leaders step up and hold those employees accountable. The low performers can either make positive improvements or be shown to the door.

Well, that's how it's supposed to work. It doesn't always happen that way. How you respond to these unmotivated salespeople sends a loud and clear message to the rest of your team. *Especially* the top performers.

According to brain theory, we have an incentive to repeat the behaviors for which we are rewarded. In our no-accountability Sales scenario, poor performers are essentially being rewarded with a paycheck and continued employment for doing the bare minimum. Here's the message they receive: No one is complaining, so why not continue to slack off?

In the meantime, who is doing the extra work? Picking up the slack? Fixing the problems? Finishing the leftover projects? Leaders usually turn to the people they can always count on: *those reliable, consistent, and amazing top performers who know how to get things done.*

Over time, the message to the Sales superstars is quite different. The reward for being efficient, conscientious team players is extra work and longer hours. That doesn't sound fair. At all. And when the unfairness of the situation becomes completely intolerable, they turn in their notice. Most leaders would never intentionally set out to overburden their team superstars, but it still happens. Slowly. Over time. With devastating impact on performance, morale, and turnover.

As a Sales leader, it all comes back to accountability. If you want to keep your top performers, quit ignoring the slackers. Set expectations. Define the rewards for meeting goals, as well as the consequences for not meeting them. Follow up and follow through. That's the best way to position yourself as a strong, credible leader who shows respect for ALL of your employees.

SALES LEADERSHIP TAKEAWAY

Hold all of your salespeople accountable for meeting clearly established goals. Think about how your rewards and responses will reinforce their behaviors — and which ones you want repeated. Most of all, make sure your top performers aren't being penalized for carrying more of the load.

12

QUIT

IGNORING DYSFUNCTION.

———————

Existing as part of a dysfunctional Sales team is just as damaging as being part of a dysfunctional family. When salespeople are trying to work in a place where it's difficult to do their jobs the right way, the organization will suffer from a cascade of negative outcomes. Problems are ignored. The wrong people are rewarded. And your top salespeople quickly become disengaged, complacent, and unmotivated. Dysfunction is like a disease that slowly but surely decimates even the best Sales teams.

One point of distinction here. We're not talking about dysfunction in work CULTURE, which represents the desired character and values of a company established over time. We're talking about dysfunction as a byproduct of workplace CLIMATE – a reflection of the "here and now." It is directly measured by how your salespeople feel about where they work, who they work for, and whether they are proud of their organizations, management, and products.

Many Sales leaders are surprised to find out that climate is, in fact, one of the biggest drivers in determining the ROI and productivity level of an organization. It's also usually one of the last things to be discussed when trying to understand why the previous years' sales were atrocious. Never ignore the direct link: *Climate determines performance.*

To assess whether your work climate is supporting or detracting from team performance, ask yourself some pointed questions. Do your salespeople really enjoy coming to work? Do they respect the team? Do they trust you as a leader? Do they feel like they have a purpose? Do they feel valued? Do they feel appreciated for their contributions? Do they feel engaged and committed to the team, the company, and their customers? It's up to you to find the weak link:

a. **The people.** Are there too many dysfunctional salespeople on your team who are making life miserable for the rest?

b. **The environment.** Are you responsible for allowing them to work in an unhealthy, chaotic, disengaged environment that makes people dread coming in to the office?

c. **The leaders.** Are your salespeople underperforming because of an unhealthy, disrespectful, or incompetent leadership team that makes their jobs more difficult?

Try to identify the prevailing climate among your team members. While leaders can work for years to make shifts in corporate culture, you can do something about a dysfunctional climate TODAY. Starting now. Remove the obstacles, and make the changes that matter.

SALES LEADERSHIP TAKEAWAY

Acknowledge whatever is creating dysfunction in the work climate for your Sales team. Fix it! Make it right – or make it better. The ball's in your court, and it's your job to take action.

13
QUIT
OVERSTATING THE NEED TO MOTIVATE ALL SALESPEOPLE.

Sales motivation is a trendy topic. Google it, and you'll find thousands of articles, workshops, and videos designed to get your Sales teams revved up and ready to go. Many times when we are invited to speak to Sales audiences, the organizers ask us to "motivate as well as educate."

Clearly, companies believe that their salespeople can't maintain or increase their momentum without ongoing motivational input. Like frothy espresso shots of enthusiasm that have to be replaced every time they wear off.

After working with hundreds of thousands of salespeople, we have a slightly different slant on the concept of Sales team motivation. It may surprise you. The truly amazing salespeople we've met don't really need or want an inspirational ticker-tape parade at every meeting or conference. They expect more of themselves than anyone else ever could. They always have. It's just how they're wired.

So if you have high performers on your team, the solution is pretty easy. Support them, remove obstacles, and watch them grow the business like nobody else can! Instead of supplying a steady stream of motivational messages, here are three ways you can provide meaningful support to fuel your top performers for even greater results:

a. **Invest in them.** In many organizations, the top-performing salespeople don't seem to need any help, so they get the least amount of development options. Would a professional sports team treat its elite players like that? No! Continue investing in your top performers so they can continue growing and improving.

b. **Reward them.** Top performers should be the highest-paid people on your team. Stop worrying about their huge commissions or bonuses. The more they make, the more you make. Find new and creative ways to reward them, and you'll be amazed by their production.

c. **Give them opportunities.** Nobody loves a challenge like top performers. Being the best person on the Sales team is probably not their ultimate goal. Be deliberate about providing them with new opportunities, new responsibilities, and new obstacles to overcome.

SALES LEADERSHIP TAKEAWAY

Set the stage for self-motivated salespeople to thrive. Instead of wasting time and money on external attempts to raise their spirits, hire the right people and create an environment that encourages them to draw from their own deeply rooted sense of motivation.

14

QUIT

FORGETTING THAT YOU ARE A COACH.

How would you describe your primary job as a Sales leader: Manager? Strategist? Decision-Maker? Nope. Hands down, your number one job needs to be *coaching*. There is no better use of your time than working with your team members to make them better at what they do. Not spending time with clients. Not networking. Not meeting with the Executive Committee.

Research shows that coaching your team members is THE most effective way to increase performance, boost the bottom line, and retain top Sales talent. Which explains why one of our biggest pet peeves is Sales leaders who don't coach. That includes those who rarely coach, as well as those who fully intend to coach but perpetually cancel and reschedule their sessions.

If you want your team to succeed, you have to coach them. Not ALL of them, by the way. The top producers may not need as much of your time. The slackers may not care. But for the right salespeople, your coaching could dramatically elevate their performance. Here are five strategies to help you enhance the way you coach your salespeople.

a. **Prove that you are worthy of being a coach.** Earn their respect by demonstrating your Sales expertise. They want to follow the lead of someone with a solid track record.

b. **Build your own skills.** Coaching isn't a performance review, an accountability discussion, or a cheerleading session. It's a skill-driven, strategy-based effort to accelerate productivity. Invest the time to learn how to coach effectively.

c. **Set the expectations.** Tell your team members that you are fully committed to coaching sessions with them on a continual basis. Explain the potential value, and tell them you welcome the opportunity to engage one-on-one.

d. **Make it a priority.** Set the date and time for coaching sessions, and schedule around them. Unless you have a dire emergency, don't cancel. Treat them like appointments with the CEO – meetings you would never move or double book.

e. **Listen carefully.** Coaching is a conversation in which leaders should spend more time listening than talking. If you let them share their wins with you, they'll feel more comfortable sharing their problems and limitations.

When you commit to coaching your team, you'll quickly form stronger connections with your salespeople. Plus, you'll see them develop and succeed in unimaginable ways.

SALES LEADERSHIP TAKEAWAY

Commit to regular coaching as a top priority. Sales leaders who emphasize coaching will witness incredible growth within their teams and in the number of deals they successfully close.

LEADERSHIP BEHAVIORS...
THAT SEND THE WRONG MESSAGE

Your salespeople are watching every move you make. Are they seeing something that inspires success?

QUIT
MULTI-TASKING.

If you're a Sales leader, your to-do list is usually jam-packed. People to manage and mentor. Customers with requests and problems to be solved. Senior executives waiting for your updates. And, of course, you have your *own* work to do.

That's when the temptation to multi-task floats by, like a welcoming life raft in a vast ocean of projects. Why do one thing when you can do three at the same time? For years, people believed that was the secret to achieving true success. Many people still believe that – and it's completely, utterly wrong.

Research has now proven that mental functions happen *one at a time*. The brain focuses on a single task. Then it flips in a split-second to focus on another. Back and forth. Back and forth. From the outside, we might appear to be handling projects simultaneously, but it's an illusion.

The outer façade says, *"I'm effortlessly efficient,"* while the inner subconscious is bouncing around and exploding like microwave popcorn. And that burning smell? It's your brain on overload. To maximize Sales leader success, you've got to give up on the myth of multi-tasking.

a. **Commit to one thing at a time.** Let go of the need to text, watch a training video, sign the quarterly evaluations, and email the meeting agenda while eating lunch at your desk. You simply can't do all of that with any sense of accuracy, efficiency, or quality.

b. **Choose to be present.** When you multi-task, no one gets your full attention. Everyone around you gets a little, disorganized slice of your brain's bandwidth. That makes people feel unimportant. And honestly, it's kind of rude. Stop and be completely present for the people who need your advice, guidance, and leadership.

c. **Consider the impact on your image.** What do others see when you are gasping for air in the middle of the multi-tasking quagmire? Chances are, you aren't projecting the image of a calm, poised, competent leader. You probably look frantic, stressed, and chaotic. If you constantly multi-task, your salespeople won't want to emulate you or follow you.

d. **Think about the health factor.** Multi-tasking is often the outward display of an anxious, self-critical mind that is terrified of falling behind. That usually comes along with increased heart rate and cortisol levels that can have devastating, long-term effects. Slow down. Take a deep breath.

SALES LEADERSHIP TAKEAWAY

Stop trying to multi-task. Take better care of yourself and those around you. Applaud yourself for finishing one thing before you start another, and give your salespeople a leader who values the quality of interactions rather than a to-do list with everything crossed off.

2

QUIT

BELIEVING EVERYONE WAS
MEANT TO BE IN SALES.

The toughest job of any Sales leader is dealing with team members who just can't seem to make the grade. They struggle to get appointments. Can't close deals. Never hit their Sales goals. Despite all of your efforts to train and coach them, you just can't seem to help them rally to produce meaningful results.

That's a bummer on two levels. First, they are dragging down the overall Sales numbers for the team. And second, you start to take it personally. After all, you're a spectacular Sales manager, not to mention a wonderful human being, right? Why can't you inspire and energize these slow starters? It's an express ticket for a major guilt trip. And, even worse, lost business.

Brace yourself for some radical truth. As amazing as you might be, you simply don't have the power, talents, and abilities to MAKE someone else successful at Sales. That has to be an inside job. Only the Sales professionals themselves can do it. The realization that follows could be difficult to discuss: Some people simply aren't suited for a career in Sales.

If your salespeople are underperforming, respond by using these three strategies:

a. **Review your own performance.** Have you done your job in clearly communicating goals and expectations? Provided resources? Coached, trained, and mentored? Held them accountable? Offered appropriate rewards and consequences? The buck stops with you! If your team isn't producing, look first for ways you can improve your own leadership.

b. **Find the heart of the problem.** Is this a skills/knowledge problem (are they *unable* to do the job)? Or is it an attitude/ambition/commitment problem (are they *unwilling* to do the job)? Identify the issue so you can effectively address it.

c. **Take action.** Once you know where the process is breaking down, make changes. If your salespeople lack skills, guide them through the development process. If they lack the motivation to learn, that's your cue to encourage them to pursue other opportunities better suited to their particular strengths and talents.

SALES LEADERSHIP TAKEAWAY

Accept that you can't transform every employee into a Sales superstar. Make sure your own skills as a coach and mentor are up to date. But also remember that you can't fix a lack of discipline, ambition, or drive. If salespeople aren't both WILLING and ABLE to do their jobs, encourage them to find one that is a better fit. Everyone will be happier.

QUIT
WASTING TIME.

———

Sales managers love to tell us they don't have enough time to get all their work done. We get it. They're expected to attend "urgent" meetings, go on calls with their salespeople, monitor selling behavior, and manage Sales reports. It's their job to keep the CRM updated. To complete the regulatory reports. And, obviously, to lead their Sales teams. Most of these ultra-busy professionals also tell us their goal is to transform their busy schedules into more productive ones.

Prepare for a shocker: *Time can't be managed.* You can only manage the way you handle the time you're given. Here are a few strategies to help you become a more effective Sales leader and reclaim any wasted time you desperately want to get back:

a. **Organize your calendar.** If you don't control your calendar, things can quickly get out of hand. For example, writing this book together required careful coordination between us. We had strict deadlines to meet. Otherwise it would be too easy for everything else to get in the way. If you become a slave to a jumbled and disorganized calendar, you'll end up overbooked, overworked, and overstressed.

b. **Prioritize your day.** Your time is a hot commodity, and you're likely in high demand to work on multiple projects. But don't lose sight of your primary goal as a Sales leader: to create an amazing, high-producing Sales team. Are you wasting time on tasks that aren't mission-critical? Keep that in the forefront as you decide what to do first each day.

c. **Be prepared for the unexpected.** Resist the urge to over-plan your time, and save some free spots on your calendar. Something will always come up that needs your attention. If your goal is time efficiency, build in a contingency plan.

d. **Streamline the meetings you control.** How can you make team meetings more productive? Could they be shorter? Are they really necessary? Get organized with an agenda, and stick to it. Every minute your salespeople are sitting in your meetings, they are losing out on precious time to sell.

e. **Get better at delegation.** Stop accepting every problem as your own. Discern when it's better to assign tasks to others and help them develop the skills needed to find valuable solutions on their own. Reserve your time for higher-level decision-making. That will not only help you gain the respect of your team, but also maintain your sanity.

f. **Stop procrastinating.** Putting things off only makes life worse. Just do it. Now!

SALES LEADERSHIP TAKEAWAY

Remember that time is money in Sales. Treat it with the respect it deserves, and don't waste it. To help increase sales and expand market share, give your salespeople as much of your quality time as you possibly can.

4

QUIT

THINKING YOU'RE IN CONTROL.

That's not a statement confident Sales leaders love to hear — especially those who have a take-charge, buck-stops-here attitude. But the reality is, you can't control exactly what your salespeople say and do. Whether they are productive. Or engaged. Or efficient. Or successful. Every person on your team has to make the personal choice of whether to perform at the highest level or just skate by. You can't make that decision for any of them.

Before that creates anxiety or gives you the idea that you're completely off the hook, let's talk about what you CAN control. For one thing, accountability is still firmly in your court. Don't hesitate to provide rewards for a job well done and deliver fair consequences when goals aren't met. Second, as the Sales leader, you're responsible for developing a framework that encourages your salespeople to make smart choices that will lead to outstanding results.

Here are three strategies you can use to make that happen:

a. **Create the right environment.** Have you given your team members everything they need? Have you clearly communicated the expectations, set the goals, and defined the strategies? Have you assessed their abilities and given them feedback? To create an environment of success, you are responsible for providing your salespeople with the knowledge and tools they need to achieve their goals. You set the tone.

b. **Tackle the hard conversations.** Salespeople need rich, ongoing feedback. Which is easy when they are doing great things. But you also have to be willing to have the tough conversations with the underperformers. That's information they need if they want to make improvements. As a leader, be sure you are equally skilled and committed to providing feedback that celebrates success AND corrects problems.

c. **Be willing to let go.** Just like salespeople can waste time and energy on prospects who will never convert to customers, Sales leaders can waste time and energy on salespeople who will never choose to be successful. If you've done your job to create a thriving environment, provided the right knowledge and tools, and shared honest feed-back, the rest is up to them. They make the choice to succeed. Or not. And if they don't choose to do what it takes to be successful, it's your responsibility to let the non-performers go. That's something you CAN control.

SALES LEADERSHIP TAKEAWAY

Recognize that success is a personal choice for each of your salespeople, and you can't control those decisions. You can, however, create an environment that inspires them. You can support them throughout the process as they make the choice to pursue success. But if they don't, it's your responsibility to take action.

5

QUIT

LETTING ADVERSITY OVERWHELM YOU.

Life is uncertain. Things don't always go as planned. And by virtue of your role as a Sales leader, you're guaranteed to get more than your fair share of adversity. You're basically positioned on the front line at Crisis Central every day. As a bonus, all eyes are on you. Your salespeople are watching how you ACT and REACT during difficult situations.

No pressure here, but we'll tell it to you straight up. Your success (and that of your team) depends on your ability to adapt efficiently, react sanely, recover quickly, and move forward boldly. That's a tall order right there – and it requires some serious resilience.

So what exactly is resilience? We define it as "the ability to become healthy, successful, and strong again after serious misfortune, setbacks, or significant change." The good news is, resilience is inside all of us. It's in our DNA. Imagine where we'd be if we weren't born with the skills needed to overcome disaster, to regroup, to rebuild, and to get on with life. The bad news is, we can't take advantage of that resilience if we don't learn how to tap into it and apply it when adversity comes knocking at the door.

Some Sales leaders grow and learn from their setbacks, while others collapse and never recover. What about you? How do YOU respond to adversity? Do you pull away or bounce back? Do you tough it out alone or reach out for help and support? Do you withdraw or forge ahead to find a solution? Do you become a victim or fight to come back stronger?

Experience shows that attitude and mindset make all the difference. Leaders who rely on their resilience look at misfortune as a temporary state. They believe they CAN and WILL get through it. Whatever they learn from the setback will actually propel them forward. Knowing that, they don't try to hide from adversity. They *expect* it and realize it's a necessary step on the journey to success.

There's a domino effect here, too: Resilient leaders create resilient teams. If you're strong enough to reemerge from a crisis ready to move forward, your team will follow your lead. Sales is a tough business. And, like it or not, you're a role model. Your salespeople will learn more from watching what you do than from listening to what you say. Make sure you are demonstrating how to gracefully deal with the unexpected and move past the obstacles.

SALES LEADERSHIP TAKEAWAY

Don't allow adversity to overwhelm you. Stay calm, and draw from your natural reservoir of resilience. Your team will notice your reactions — calm and controlled or angry and irrational — and will follow your example, for better or worse.

6

QUIT
PERPETUATING THE SILO MENTALITY.

———————

For the salesperson perspective on this chapter, see page 11 in the reverse side of the book.

Healthy companies need structure, and organizing internally by business teams with similar roles and objectives can vastly improve efficiency. Makes sense. The processes and procedures you enforce in the Sales department probably don't apply to your counterparts in Finance. By creating those silos, companies give different groups of people the unique tools they need to boost their own flexibility.

The problem occurs when the people within those valuable silos begin to perceive the metaphorical walls surrounding their departments as actual, airtight barriers. Consider the impact this type of thinking could have on your salespeople. Their individual Sales quotas and team goals could begin to feel more important than the organization's broader mission. Communication with other departments might grind to a halt. Collaboration fizzles. Information and ideas are no longer shared across lines of business.

Needless to say, the silo mentality can be deadly for Sales teams — and it's your job as the Sales leader to break that down. Here are several strategies to get you started.

a. **Find the source of the silo mentality.** Dysfunction across departmental lines often starts with conflicted leaders who purposely create strong boundaries between groups. Does the problem start with upper management? Could you be perpetuating it? Find the source. Then become a champion for changing the perception of these cross-silo relationships. Demonstrate how they can be collaboratively profitable rather than competitively destructive.

b. **Build bridges.** Begin developing strong, interdepartmental relationships that can strategically help you and your Sales team improve your impact on the customer experience. Invite other departments to connect, collaborate, and cooperate with your team. Make the first move to break down the barriers.

c. **Increase the information flow.** Start to create processes and systems that enable and encourage communication across silos to benefit your salespeople. Plan meetings to facilitate that. Create an online portal for idea generation and sharing. Reward and recognize team members who make the effort to work across lines of business.

SALES LEADERSHIP TAKEAWAY

Accept that business silos may be necessary, but do your part throughout the organization to banish the silo mentality that creates an unhealthy environment. You can help your salespeople see the benefits of collaboration and communication with other parts of your company as a way to bring more value to the table for their customers.

7

QUIT

OVERLOOKING CHANGES
IN THE SALES ENVIRONMENT.

We both know one thing for sure: The Sales industry is totally different than it was five years ago. In some cases, even one year ago. And yet so many Sales managers are leading exactly the same way as they always have. That's a huge problem when you consider the massive scope of change involved. Everything is different. The products. The customers. The competition. The way we gather information. The way we make decisions. As a Sales leader, if you aren't prepared for that, you're sending your salespeople out to fight a battle they will never win.

How long has it been since you last changed your Sales strategy? Are you listening to your customers to understand whether your products are still working for them? Are you tuned in when your salespeople explain why they are suddenly struggling to compete? Ignoring change is a major Sales hazard. If your strategies and techniques are out of date, take action NOW!

To guide that process, try following these steps:

a. **Pay attention.** Remind yourself to look outside of your company and think about the changes happening around you. Is the economy shifting? Have new competitors popped up? How is the online world making an impact on what you sell and how you sell it? Change can be a daunting obstacle when you don't see it coming. But if you recognize it and plan for it, change can become a major opportunity. Refuse to bury your head in the sand.

b. **Be relentless in gathering information.** Invest the time to learn more from your salespeople. Ask them what is working and what falls flat. Where are they repeatedly encountering objections? What needs to change? Ask customers how they are buying, where they get their information, how they make their decisions, and what trends they are noticing. Pose those targeted questions, and then listen. Really listen.

c. **Take risks.** Shake it up! Be willing to break out of the rut and try something new. Granted, new approaches don't always work, but you'll never know until you try. No risk, no reward.

Whatever Sales strategies your team used to achieve success last year may not automatically work again this year. Maybe. Maybe not. But instead of hiding from change or pretending it isn't happening, make it your mission to seek it out. Ride the wave of change instead of trying to swim upstream and fighting it with every breath you take.

SALES LEADERSHIP TAKEAWAY

Embrace the reality of change. Pursue it. Make sure your salespeople are prepared to succeed in the new environment, because ignoring change is a sure way to lose sales and lose clients.

8

QUIT
FORGETTING TO OWN IT.

———

If we had to name the top three complaints Sales leaders have about their teams, apathy would be at the top of the list. *"They lack drive."* *"They're just going through the motions."* Managers who make those comments are often surprised when we respond by suggesting they take a long, hard look in the mirror. That's right. Lack of engagement is a leadership issue, not an employee issue. Leaders have to own this one.

Let's break that down. As a Sales leader, you need to take responsibility for more than just handing out goals and making sure they are met. It's your job to get your team members on board with whatever you are trying to accomplish. If they hit road-blocks, it's your job to help remove them. If they need additional support, it's your job to get it. And if there's a problem with the team, it's your job to solve it.

You might be leading the smartest and most independent salespeople in the world, but that still doesn't justify a detached, hands-off approach to leadership. Their level of engagement will directly determine the scope of their Sales success. And their level of engagement (or lack of it) is directly determined by you. End of story.

Here are four ways you can inspire engagement within your Sales team by taking ownership of your role as a leader.

a. **Define the bigger purpose.** Give your salespeople context and show them how they are part of something bigger. Explain the reasons why it matters if they reach their goals. What will it mean for them? For the team? For the company? What they do makes a difference. Help them to connect the dots.

b. **Give them some skin in the game.** People support what they help to create. As a Sales leader, move past telling your team members WHAT goals to meet and start asking them HOW they will do it. That gives them a voice. Responsibility. A sense of ownership.

c. **Provide support.** Teams that are highly engaged feel thoroughly supported. You can create that atmosphere by helping them build their skills. Coaching them. Making sure they have the tools and resources they need. Invest in them, and they will invest in you.

d. **Hold them accountable.** Reward great performance. Be the first to tell them when they are doing well. More importantly, make them toe the line when they aren't.

SALES LEADERSHIP TAKEAWAY

Take responsibility for keeping your salespeople engaged. Own it! As the leader, it's your job to build enthusiasm and commitment along the path to reaching (and exceeding) goals.

9

QUIT

BEING AFRAID TO
GET YOUR HANDS DIRTY.

Ever called in for tech support on some trendy gadget and gotten connected to someone who has clearly never seen the product before? This person is enthusiastically reading from a script and telling you exactly how to fix the problem. And yet, it's obvious the representative has no clue.

That's what it's like when salespeople report to leaders who sit behind their desks and talk about Sales without ever actually doing it. The managers tell them what to do and how to do it, but it all sounds a bit hollow. Ask yourself: When was the last time you tried to make a sale? Or went on a call with one of your team members? Or lost a deal to the competition? Or tried to sell in a shifting economy? If you're coaching without doing, then guess what? Your salespeople aren't listening.

From our years of working with Sales organizations, we can tell you one thing for sure: The strongest Sales leaders are the ones who can actually sell. They understand the importance of getting out from behind their desks and trying to land a deal on occasion. So if you're not experiencing the vast industry changes from your salespeople's perspectives, you can't lead them effectively. They need to know you understand their world, and they need to know you can do what you are asking them to do.

If you are spending more time shuffling paperwork than trying to increase your own Sales acumen, here are three strategies to help you reengage with your craft and get your hands a little dirty.

a. **Take the lead.** At least once a month, set up your own Sales call. Ask one of your high-performing salespeople to join you. Demonstrate that you're working just as hard as they are to sell. Then discuss the meeting over lunch.

b. **Tag along.** Go on Sales calls with your team members. Ride with them as they go out to visit customers, and help them analyze their prospect lists. Seeing them handle the Sales process "live" will give you an opportunity to evaluate their work and provide valuable insights on how they might improve their skills. As speakers, we often invite peers to attend our performances and share their honest feedback.

c. **Work the process.** As the Sales leader, you probably developed the process by which your salespeople find leads, make calls, and follow up with customers. Test it out! Is it still effective? What needs to be changed? Take a proactive approach when it comes to evaluating the system you expect your salespeople to follow.

SALES LEADERSHIP TAKEAWAY

Immerse yourself in the Sales process to gain the respect of your team members. Show them that you fully understand the challenges they face by closing a few deals of your own.

10

QUIT
ASSUMING GREAT SALESPEOPLE MAKE GREAT LEADERS.

It's like apples and oranges. The skill set required to be a heavy-hitting, high-performing salesperson is different than the skill set required to be a supportive, team-developing leader.

Check out the striking contrast. Sales superstars love their freedom and their commission checks. The harder they work, the more money they make. Their healthy egos give them confidence and ambition to keep moving forward, despite rejection or road-blocks. They love the spotlight and the thrill of being the next one to close a huge deal.

Now imagine telling one of these extreme challengers: *"Great news! You've been promoted! Instead of going out to conquer new customers and bring in new business, you get to cheer on the people who do."* There's a fair chance that announcement won't initially be seen as a winning proposition. It's a dramatic transition to go from fiercely independent and focused on your own goals... to intricately connected and far more interested in the achievement of others. Fact is, sometimes great salespeople don't make great Sales leaders.

Perhaps you've been thrown into this new position or you're contemplating a promotion for someone on your current team. Give it some serious consideration. Here are the things to remember when leaping from salesperson to Sales leader mode:

a. **Tone down the ego.** Salespeople want someone who will fairly provide expertise, not a know-it-all.

b. **Stop selling yourself and start selling them.** It's not about you anymore. It's about your ability to create a healthy, productive team that can sell and succeed.

c. **Stay objective.** Don't try to be friends with your salespeople. Maintain some healthy separation to pave the way for potentially tough conversations in the future.

d. **Make peace with confrontation.** It's a necessary part of doing business. Instead of avoiding conflict, face it head-on and solve problems for your team and your customers.

e. **Hold your team accountable.** Don't be the leader who forgets to monitor the progress of your salespeople or refuses to take them to task if they fall short of their goals.

f. **Buck the status quo.** Recognize that part of your role as a leader is consistent improvement. Goals are no longer something to achieve but something to surpass in a bold way. Work with your team to improve performance. Never settle.

SALES LEADERSHIP TAKEAWAY

Beware of the problems that can occur when great salespeople are thrust into the world of leadership. The requirements and parameters are different. To succeed, new managers have to adjust their mindsets.

11

QUIT

FOCUSING ONLY ON RESULTS.

Don't worry. We're not about to recommend that you wrap up every Sales meeting with a group hug. But we are suggesting that you step back and think about whether the bottom line has become the singular focus for everything you say and do as a Sales leader. Making the quotas. Reaching the goals. Expanding the market share. Have you given the impression to your salespeople that the final results overshadow everything else?

Yes, results are important. But they shouldn't be the *only* priority. Your main job should really be to successfully manage the Sales behaviors of the people on your team. If you do that well, the results will take care of themselves. In fact, the more you focus on improving these behaviors, the better the results will be.

Imagine starting a fresh fiscal year with your Sales team. You vividly describe the organization's mission. You discuss the goals, and you clarify your expectations. Everyone has their marching orders, and off they go! That's a great start. But what happens next? If you wait until the numbers come in to measure the progress, you've missed the greatest opportunity to develop and grow your Sales team.

At that point, it's too late to focus on the appropriate activities that could have made a difference in the final, quantifiable outcome. It's too late to make sure the relationship-building and deal-making behaviors of your salespeople are in alignment with the end goal of developing customers for life. Salespeople can get so distracted by the goals and the quotas that they forget to develop and nurture the actions that help them reach those.

Great Sales leaders are responsible for guiding and consistently improving that process. Not just harping on the results, but helping Sales teams to develop and achieve them. Here's our seven-step plan for leaders to complete the full process:

a. Determine the desired results for your team.
b. Communicate the behaviors, activities, and performance expectations required to achieve those results.
c. Stay available as a coach, mentor, motivator, and educator.
d. Monitor and evaluate the behaviors throughout the process.
e. Hold team members accountable for what they agreed to do.
f. Provide healthy, open, constructive feedback to help salespeople improve and grow.
g. Be ready to give kudos for a job well done.

SALES LEADERSHIP TAKEAWAY

Focus on the mindsets, attitudes, and activities that will help your salespeople generate the results you want. When you support the middle part of the process, you'll be thrilled with the final outcome.

CONCLUSION

To expand your success as a Sales leader, you have to be very strategic about what you do. And, more importantly, what you don't do.

We hope the strategies in this book have inspired you to guide and support your team members in achieving their highest goals. We also hope they've encouraged you to quit doing the things that are standing in your way, such as:

Habits that guarantee an ineffective Sales team.
Behaviors that destroy your credibility.
Tactics that prevent you from motivating others.

And once you make the choice to STOP doing those things? You'll START moving forward at an unprecedented pace, providing serious momentum for your Sales team to step up production and exceed even the most ambitious goals.

By applying these strategies, you'll be able to identify and hire superior Sales talent. Create a winning work environment that fosters greater engagement. Coach your salespeople to reach their full potential. Build stronger teams through trust and accountability. Respond to adversity and change with the poise of a revered role model. And, best of all, lead your team to sell with phenomenally high rates of success.

You may have intuitively known about some of these leadership behaviors and attitudes that could be holding you back. Or you have learned about them the hard way, by having the wrong salespeople on your team or inadvertently allowing a climate of dysfunction. But we're betting you also uncovered some hidden opportunities for improvement. Some new leadership strategies you'd never considered before. Some fresh insights that could change the game for your career trajectory.

We hope this book has given you the exact fuel you need to reassess your current approach, replenish your enthusiasm, and rediscover your passion for the exciting challenges of Sales leadership.

If you want to be the kind of Sales leader who is known for record-breaking, quota-blasting, off-the-charts wins, make the commitment to adopt this new approach. Cut through the obstacles, and you'll be well on your way to creating a killer Sales team.

How cool is that?!?

ABOUT
Meridith Elliott Powell

Named one of the *Top 15 Business Growth Experts To Watch* by *CurrencyFair,* Meridith is a highly acclaimed business growth expert, keynote speaker, and award-winning author. She coaches leaders to learn the Sales and growth strategies needed to help their organizations succeed, no matter what happens with the economy.

Known for her innovative content, wicked wit and high-energy style, Meridith was recently voted **One of the Top Motivational Speakers to Energize Sales Teams** by *Resourceful Selling* magazine. Meridith delivers compelling keynotes that have salespeople on the edge of their seats, fully engaged and ready to produce powerful results.

Other Books

Own It: Redefining Responsibility
Winning in the Trust and Value Economy
42 Rules to Turn Prospects into Customers
Mastering the Art of Success
The Confidence Plan

Online Courses

Own It: Redefining Responsibility
Sales: Selling Financial Products and Services
Consulting Foundations: Building Your Sales System
Selling into Industries: Manufacturing
Selling into Industries: Telecommunications
Soft Skills for Sales Professionals

Connect

Email: **mere@valuespeaker.com**
Website: **www.ValueSpeaker.com**
Phone: **(888) 526-9998**

Meridith Elliott Powell, CSP
Meridith Elliott Powell
@MeridithElliottPowell
Meridith Elliott Powell

ABOUT
Connie Podesta

Connie is a Hall of Fame international keynote speaker, an award-winning author of nine books, and an expert in the Psychology of Sales and Human Behavior. Connie is known for being a game-changing, sales-generating, leadership-developing, revenue-building ball of fire. Her rare blend of laugh-out-loud humor, amazing insights, convention-defying substance and no-nonsense style have made her a consistently in-demand business and Sales speaker for more than 25 years.

Voted **One of the Top Motivational Speakers to Energize Sales Teams** by *Resourceful Selling* magazine, Connie is famous for dazzling her audiences with unforgettable, reality-based strategies that inspire them to take bold action. She also empowers these salespeople to dynamically change the way they approach every interaction, successfully taking on a new generation of customers who have more choices than ever before.

Other Books

Leadership…Like You've Never Heard It Before
10 Ways to Stand Out from the Crowd
Life Would Be Easy if it Weren't for Other People
Happiness is Serious Business
Selling to Women/Selling to Men
How to be the Person Successful Companies Would Fight to Keep
Audiences Stand Up When You Stand Out
Texting Harry

Connect

Email: **connie@conniepodesta.com**
Website: **www.ConniePodesta.com**
Phone: **(972) 596-5501**

f **Connie Podesta Presents**
in **Connie Podesta**
@Connie_Podesta
You Tube **Connie Podesta Presents**

ACKNOWLEDGEMENTS

**Content Development and Editing Services
provided by Susan Priddy**

Susan Priddy is an award-winning writer and marketing strategist who specializes in targeted business communications that generate real results. Integrating her MBA and Journalism degrees, she is known for developing powerful content infused with strategic focus and creative flair.

www.SusanPriddy.com

**Graphic Design and Layout Services
provided by Kendra Cagle**

Kendra Cagle is an award-winning graphic designer with a Bachelor of Science in Graphic Design from The Art Institute of Fort Lauderdale. She combines creative talents with a passion for art to craft original design for speakers, authors, and fellow entrepreneurs.

www.5LakesDesign.com